MARQUETTE
UNIVERSITY
PRESS

REFORMATION TEXTS
WITH TRANSLATION (1350-1650)

Kenneth Hagen, General Editor

Series: Women of the Reformation
Merry Wiesner-Hanks, Editor

Volume 1

MARQUETTE
UNIVERSITY

PRESS

Convents Confront the Reformation: Catholic and Protestant Nuns in Germany

Introduced and Edited by Merry Wiesner-Hanks

Translated by Joan Skocir and Merry Wiesner-Hanks

Association of American
University Presses

MARQUETTE UNIVERSITY PRESS
MILWAUKEE

The Association of Jesuit University Presses

Library of Congress Cataloguing-in-Publication Data

Convents confront the Reformation : Catholic and Protestant nuns in
   Germany / introduced and edited by Merry Wiesner-Hanks ; translated
   by Joan Skocir and Merry Wiesner-Hanks.
      p. cm. — (Reformation texts with translation (1350-1650).
   Women of the Reformation ; v. 1)
      Contents: Katherine Rem — Ursula of Münsterberg — Anna Sophia of
   Quedlinburg — Martha Elisabeth Zitter.
      Includes bibliographical references.
      Texts in German with English translation.
      ISBN 0-87462-702-8
      1. Nuns—Germany—Biography. 2. Ex-nuns—Germany—Biography.
   3. Reformation—Germany—Biography. 4. Monasticism and religious
   orders for women—Germany—History—16th century--Sources.
   5. Monasticism and religious orders for women—Lutheran Church—
   History—16th century—Sources. 6. Germany—Church history—16th
   century—Sources. I. Wiesner-Hanks, Merry, 1952– II. Series.
   BX4225.C64 1996
   271'.9'0092243—dc20
   [B]   96-10117

Printed in the United States of America
© Marquette University Press, 2004
First printing, 1996.
Second printing, 1998, including review and corrections
Third prining 2004
Fourth printing 2010

Table of Contents

Foreword

Reformation Texts With Translation (1350-1650) (RTT) are published by Marquette University Press, Andrew Tallon, Director. RTT are brief theological and religious works from the fourteenth through the seventeenth centuries translated into English usually for the first time.

The purpose is to provide religious works that are not easily available to those students of this period in need of primary sources and in need of maintaining the languages. We thereby seek to keep alive the tradition of *textus minores*. The criteria for the selection of texts will be solid, intellectual, and exciting material that will entice our students to dig deeper into the primary languages from the Renaissance and Reformation.

The texts are aimed at a wide audience of scholars, students, persons working in religious areas (such as churches or synagogues), as well as laymen and laywomen interested in pursuing religious readings from the Renaissance. To facilitate their use, each text features the original language and English translation on facing pages.

Latin and German will be our first languages; thereafter, French and Spanish. Since the goal is not only to make more works (from 1350 to 1650) available in translation but also to encourage scholars to continue in original language study, we first selected works in manageable Latin. For German we follow the standard pattern for modern editions of early modern German literature by modernizing the orthography but not the spelling.

Three series within RTT are currently in production: Biblical Studies, edited by Dr. Franz Posset; Women of the Reformation, edited by Prof. Merry Wiesner-Hanks; and the Late Reformation, edited by Prof. Robert Kolb.

Kenneth Hagen
General Editor

Preface

With the development of women's history over the last twenty-five years, a number of texts by women in the early modern period have been discovered, edited, translated, and published. This has deepened our understanding of women's experience in the past, and also allowed us to view major historical changes such as the Renaissance and the Reformation in new ways. The present volume is a contribution to this growing body of literature.

The four texts in this volume are all by women who resided in convents or similar institutions, or who had recently left convents, in Germany in the sixteenth and seventeenth centuries. They allow us to hear — with some filtering by their male editors and publishers — women's opinions about the merits of clerical celibacy and convent life. None of these works has been previously translated into English, and only one of them has been published in German since the early modern period. The primary purpose of this book is to make these texts available in English, but a secondary purpose is to make the German text available in a modern edition with a modern type font. In the German text, the orthography has been modernized, but the spellings have not; punctuation has occasionally been added for clarity, for early modern authors used extremely long sentences punctuated by slash marks rather than commas and semicolons.

The editor wishes to thank several people who have assisted in the development and production of this volume. Prime among these is Joan Skocir, who did several of the translations and typed much of the German text. The series editor Kenneth Hagen first proposed the idea to me, for it was his decision to include texts by women in the Reformation Texts With Translation series. Terrance Dinovo, the Curator of Special Collections at the Lutheran Brotherhood Foundation Reformation Library, helped me obtain microfilm copies of several of the works. Ulrike Strasser and Gerhild Scholz Williams provided translation assistance with particularly obscure passages, and Aldemar Hagen was an especially skillful and careful copy editor, at a time when copy-editing seems a lost art.

Merry Wiesner-Hanks
Milwaukee, Wisconsin
December 20, 1995

The Texts

One of the texts has been reprinted in a modern edition:

Ursula of Münsterberg. "Christliche Ursachen des verlassenen Klosters zu Freiberg." In *Dr. Martin Luthers Sämmtliche Werke*. 2nd ed. Edited by Johann Georg Walch, 19:1694-1723. St. Louis: Concordia Publishing House, 1907.

Three of the texts are available only in early modern editions, and are held in the collection of the Herzog August Library in Wolfenbüttel, Germany:

[Rem, Katherine]. *Antwurt Zwayer Closter frauwen im Katheriner Closter zu Augspurg/an Bernhart Remen*. Augsburg: P. Ulhart, 1523. Herzog August Bibliothek shelfmark 77.2 Theol. 4 (13).

Anna Sophia, Abbess of Quedlinburg. *Der treue Seelenfreund Christus Jesus/mit nachdenklichen Sinn-Gemahlden*. . . Jena: Georg Sengenwald, 1658. Herzog August Bibliothek shelfmark 915.2 Theol. (3).

Zitter, Martha Elisabeth. *Grundlichen Ursachen welche Jungfer Martha Elisabeth Zitterin bewogen das Franntzosiche alias Weiss-Frauenkloster in Errfurt/Ursuliner Ordens/zuverlassen/und sich zu der waaren Evangelischen Religion zu bekennen*. Jena: 1678. Herzog August Bibliothek shelfmark K104 Helm 8 (4).

The texts by Katherine Rem and Martha Zitter are also held in the Lutheran Brotherhood Foundation Reformation Research Library, a microform collection of primary sources dealing with the religious and social aspects of the Reformation movement from 1500 to 1650. It is housed in the Rare Book Room on the campus of Luther Seminary, St. Paul, Minnesota. Access to the collection is through the Research Library Information Network (RLIN: Library identifier MNLT).

Introduction

Toward the end of his life, after he had been teaching church history for over 50 years, the well-known Reformation scholar Roland Bainton turned his attention from the men who had transformed religion in the sixteenth century to the women who had assisted them and opposed them. He published three books, *Women of the Reformation in Germany and Italy, Women of the Reformation in France and England,* and *Women of the Reformation from Spain to Scandinavia.*[1] In many ways these mark the beginning of scholarship on women and the Reformation, and they also reflect the state of women's history during the early 1970s, the initial period of its recent expansion. The earliest studies of women — including Bainton's — tended to be biographical and focused on great women, on "women worthies" as the early modern historian Natalie Zemon Davis has termed them. Bainton's books, for example, are biographical sketches mostly of queens, noblewomen, and wives of prominent reformers. These women shaped the Reformation largely through their influence on their husbands or their position as rulers of territories during times of religious turmoil.

In the twenty-five years since Bainton's first book was published, women's history has matured as a field. The kinds of women now studied by historians are no longer simply "women worthies," but are also ordinary women living normal lives and ordinary women acting in extraordinary ways. The kinds of questions historians now ask are no longer simply "What did women contribute to such-and-such an event?" but also "What did this event mean for women of different classes and races? How was women's experience different from men's? How did women perceive things differently from men, and differently from other women?" To answer these questions, historians have both used well-known sources in new ways and discovered new sources which reveal women's experiences.

This book is an outgrowth of the search for new sources which reveal the experience of women during the Reformation period. It includes all or parts of four works, three of which have not been reprinted since their original publication in the sixteenth or seventeenth centuries, and none of which has been previously translated into English. All of them were written entirely or in part by women, and by women of a particular type — those who were, or who had

until recently been, residents in a convent or other type of religious house. The first two date from the 1520s, the earliest years of the Reformation, and the second two from the mid-seventeenth century, after the Thirty Years War had ended and the religious division of Germany was set.

The first work is a letter of Katherine Rem of the Katherine convent in Augsburg to her brother Bernard — and an excerpt from his answer to her and to his daughter, who was also in the convent — printed in Augsburg in 1523. The second is a letter of Ursula of Münsterberg to her cousins Dukes George and Heinrich of Saxony, explaining why she left the convent of Mary Magdalene the Penitent in Freiberg, first printed in 1528 and later reprinted with an afterword by Luther. The third source is selections from a book of meditations, *Der treue Seelenfreund Christus Jesus*, written by the Lutheran abbess of Quedlinburg, Anna Sophia, the daughter of the Duke of Hesse, first published in Jena in 1658. The final source is a pamphlet written by Martha Elisabeth Zitter describing reasons for leaving the Ursuline convent in Erfurt, printed in Jena in 1678.

Why focus on women in religious houses? One answer to this question is a very practical one: Convent residents, especially professed nuns, were much more likely to be literate than laywomen, so were more likely to leave a record of their experiences and thoughts. The institutions in which nuns lived were accustomed to women writing, so were less likely to discard their writings than were lay families or the people to whom women wrote letters. (As an example of this we find that many letters from Luther to his wife Katherine von Bora have survived, but none from her to him.) Convent residents, particularly abbesses and other women in positions of power, were often members of prominent local noble families, so their words were seen as important for the same reasons that those of a queen or secular noblewomen were.

There are other reasons besides the purely practical one of the survival of sources to focus on women in convents, however. Women religious often made up as much as five to ten percent of the population in many German cities, so that they were a significant share of the female population. The Protestant rejection of celibacy and monastic vows had a great impact on women religious, both cloistered nuns and women who lived in less formal religious communities such as Beguines and Franciscan tertiaries. One of the first moves of an

area rejecting Catholicism was to close the monasteries and convents, either confiscating the buildings and land immediately or forbidding new novices and allowing the current residents to live out their lives on a portion of the convent's old income. In England and Ireland, where all monasteries and convents were taken over by the Crown, most nuns got very small pensions and were expected to return to their families, though not all did. Many Irish nuns fled to religious communities on the continent or continued to fulfill their religious vows in hiding while they waited for the chance to emigrate. In many cities of the Netherlands, the convents were closed, their assets liquidated, and the women given their dowries and a pension. In most Protestant areas of Germany, convents and monasteries were either closed outright and the residents ordered to move to a Catholic area, or the current residents were allowed to continue living there but no new novices accepted. Convent lands and buildings were confiscated, with the buildings often turned into hospitals or schools.

Histories of the Reformation have long reported this closing of religious houses, but until recently have made little distinction between men's and women's houses. They have described how monks often left their monasteries and became pastors in the new Protestant churches, but have not explored what happened to the women who may have been forced to leave their convents, for whom there was no place in the Protestant clergy. How did women religious respond to the Protestant rejection of celibacy in the first decades of the Reformation?

The first two sources reprinted here address that question. As you will see, Katherine Rem defended her way of life and Ursula of Münsterberg chose to leave the convent. Both of these models were followed by many other women. The most prominent example of a nun who left her convent was Katherine von Bora, who fled to the Luther household and became Luther's wife.[2] The most prominent example of one who fought to stay was Charitas Pirckheimer, the abbess of the St. Clara convent in Nuremberg and sister of the humanist Willibald Pirckheimer, who described in vivid detail the ways in which young women were violently dragged out of the convent by their parents while city residents shouted insults: "The children cried that they did not want to leave the pious, holy convent, that they were absolutely not in hell, but if they broke out of it they would descend into the abyss of hell. . . . The three children screamed in a

single voice, 'We don't want to be freed of our vows, rather we want to keep our vows to God with his help.'"[3]

The religious houses in Germany which fought the Reformation most vigorously were generally those whose leading residents were members of local noble families. Since their foundings in the early and high middle ages, many convents had been open only to members of the nobility and were thus socially exclusive; lower-class women might be associated with a convent as lay sisters to do the harder physical labor or routine maintenance, but they could not become professed nuns. The abbesses of these convents controlled large amounts of property and often had jurisdiction over many subjects. Though every convent had to have a priest available to say mass and hear confessions because the Catholic church ruled these were functions which no woman could perform, all of the other administrative duties and much of the spiritual counseling of novices and residents were carried out by women.

Some of what I have been calling convents were technically canoness houses *(Kanonissenstifte)*, following the Institutio Sanctimonialum Aquisgranensis, the Aachen Rule of 816 as their rule rather than the stricter Benedictine or Augustinian rules. In houses that followed the Institutio Aquisgranensis, women could own personal property and have their own quarters; they also took no solemn vows and could thus leave the house if they chose. Though the difference is important, it was also often blurred as canoness houses enforced policies more strict than their rule, convents neglected to enforce their rules and so looked more like canoness houses, or as houses of both types switched from one rule to another. The leader in both houses was generally called an abbess *(Abtissin)*, which further muddies the issue. Though one might have thought Protestant authorities would have made a clear distinction between the two — canonesses did not take vows, and much Protestant anti-monastic literature concentrates on the evils of monastic vows — they did not, ordering canoness houses to be closed just as readily as convents. Some canoness houses were more successful than convents at opposing closure, but this resulted more from the family connections of their noble residents than from a recognition that they were not actually convents.

The high point of many religious houses in terms of political power and intellectual accomplishments was the tenth and eleventh centuries, when abbesses of what were termed double monasteries were

often in charge of monks as well as nuns, and when Hroswitha of Gandersheim wrote the first original dramas since the end of the Roman Empire for the women in her house. (Gandersheim was a canoness house, so Hroswitha is technically not a nun, though she is often referred to as such.) In the late eleventh century, a drive for reform led the church to dissolve double monasteries and enforce stricter enclosure for all nuns, which reduced the abbesses' power and visibility in the surrounding community. Canoness houses were pressured to become convents, though the wishes of noble families to keep their daughters eligible for marriage often led such houses to adopt very loose rules; though the houses followed the Benedictine Rule, they did not demand solemn vows, further blurring the distinction between nuns and canonesses. Religious houses in general, both male and female, lost their place as the main intellectual centers of Europe, replaced by universities, which were closed to women. In their writings and in their spiritual life, nuns and canonesses in the late middle ages turned to mysticism and personal devotions, rather than giving political advice or writing plays for public performance.

By the fifteenth century, it appeared to some church officials and the more rigorous nuns as if many religious houses had forgotten their spiritual focus. In many ways this is not surprising, as some convent residents were not there willingly but had been placed in a convent by their parents because the cost of a dowry for marriage was too high; the entrance fees demanded by convents were generally lower than the dowry which a husband of one's own social class would expect. Such nuns often continued to live as they would outside the convent, not even following the more lenient rule expected of canonesses — they wore secular clothing and jewelry, entertained visitors, ate fancy food, retained servants, and frequently left the convent to visit family or friends. In many areas of Europe, leaders of the orders with which convents were affiliated or reform-minded abbesses attempted to halt such behavior and enforce strict rules of conduct and higher standards of spirituality. These fifteenth-century reforms had both positive and negative results for women religious. On the negative side, they often put religious houses more closely under the control of a local male bishop, taking away some of the abbess's independent power, and decreased the contact which the women had with the outside world, which also decreased their opportunities to get donations. On the positive side, they often built up a strong sense of

group cohesion among the residents and gave them a greater sense of the spiritual worth of their lives, particularly if an abbess herself had led the reform.

Long traditions of power, independence, and prestige combined with a reinvigorated spiritual life to make reformed convents and canoness houses the most vocal and resolute opponents of the Protestant Reformation. This was recognized by their contemporaries, as, for example, a papal nuncio who reported that "the four women's convents [in Magdeburg] have remained truer to their beliefs and vows than the men's monasteries, who have almost all fallen away."[4] When Duke Ernst of Brunswick, who had been trained at the University of Wittenberg, began to introduce the Reformation in his territories in the 1520s, almost all of the male monasteries agreed with very little pressure to disband and give their property to the duke, but all of the female convents in his territories refused even to listen to Protestant preachers. In two of these, Walsrode and Medingen, the nuns locked the convent door and took refuge in the choir of the chapel; Duke Ernst first pleaded with them personally, then ordered the gates forcibly opened and a hole bashed in the choir for his Protestant preachers to speak through.[5] In another convent in Lüne, the nuns lit old felt slippers to drive out the preacher with smoke, sang during his sermons, and when ordered to be quiet did their rosaries. They were forbidden to hold public mass, and so they held it in their private quarters or the convent granary.[6] The nuns in Heiningen refused to give any food to the Protesant preachers sent to the convent, hiding whatever they had, and none gave in to ducal pressure to leave, despite promises of a twenty gulden dowry.[7]

The visitations accompanying the Reformation in the bishoprics of Magdeburg and Halberstadt found many nuns able to argue very skillfully in favor of their Catholic beliefs. The abbess at Althaldensleben, for example, pointed out that if she had accepted the first Protestant teachings introduced into the convent, she would now be branded a Philippist — a follower of Philipp Melanchthon whose ideas were opposed by many other Lutheran leaders in the late sixteenth century — and would have to change her beliefs again. As she was uncertain about what further changes the Protestants might make, she preferred to stay with the old Catholic teachings.[8] The nuns' determination had social and political as well as religious roots, however, for they recognized that as women they could have no office

in any Protestant church; the role of a pastor's wife was an unthinkable decrease in status for a woman of noble standing.

In some territories of central Germany, the women's firmness combined with other religious and political factors to allow many houses to survive for centuries as Catholic establishments within Protestant territories. In the bishoprics of Magdeburg and Halberstadt, which became Protestant, half of the female convents survived, but only one-fifth of the monasteries. Some of this was certainly due to the women's zeal noted by papal nuncio, but also to the fact that religious and political authorities did not think the women's institutions were as great a threat as the men's. The marriage market for upper-class women also played a role. The cost of dowries was rising in early modern Germany, and even wealthy families could often not afford to marry off all their daughters to appropriate partners. As six noblemen wrote to one of the Dukes of Brunswick when he was contemplating closing the convents in his territory put it, "What would happen to our sisters' and relatives' honor and our reputation if they are forced to marry renegade monks, cobblers, and tailors?"[9] And the men writing were *Lutheran* nobles!

Some houses also survived as religious institutions by accepting Lutheran theology except for its rejection of the monastic life. Abbesses took to heart Luther's early teachings on the possibility of a truly Christian convent life, which were also expressed in statements of faith such as the Wittenberg Articles of 1536: "If certain persons of outstanding character, capable of living a life under a rule, feel a desire to pass their lives in the cloister, we do not wish to forbid them, so long as their doctrine and worship remain pure."[10] They then reformed the territories under their control, but kept their own convents open. Anna von Stolberg, for example, the abbess of the free imperial canoness house of Quedlinburg, governed a sizable territory including nine churches and two male monasteries. When she became Protestant in the 1540s she made all priests swear to Luther's Augsburg Confession and turned her Franciscan monastery into an elementary school for both boys and girls, an interesting gender reversal of the usual pattern of male authorities transforming female convents into schools or using convent property to fund (male, of course) scholars at universities. She continued to receive both imperial and papal privileges, for Catholic authorities were unwilling to cut off support from what was, at any rate, still more or less a *con-*

vent. She was also not uniformly criticized by Lutheran leaders, however, who emphasized that she was, at any rate, *Lutheran.* Quedlinburg was not the only religious house in this situation. At least fourteen convents in the relatively small territory of Brunswick/Lüneburg survived into the nineteenth century by becoming Lutheran, most of which are still Protestant religious establishments for unmarried women today.

Though there was support for monastic life in some of Luther's writings and in some Protestant documents, there was also harsh criticism in many Protestant works, so that women who chose to live in Lutheran convents often felt the need to justify their decisions. As you will read in the third selection reprinted here, Anna Sophia of Quedlinburg defended her life eloquently. This work was regarded as theologically suspect by some Lutheran theologians, who thought she stressed the ubiquity of Christ's presence too strongly in her comment that women could feel this presence equally with men. It was later judged acceptable, however, and was reprinted several times.[11]

The study of women's religious establishments during the Reformation period is only beginning, and at this point it is very difficult to determine how many convents or other types of religious houses throughout Germany were able to survive as either Catholic or Protestant institutions. It is sometimes even difficult to tell what their religious affiliation was at any particular point. Lüne, for instance, was forced to accept a Protestant ordinance in 1555, which declared that the convent was now an educational center *(Ausbildungsstätte)* for women; but the women wore Benedictine habits and described themselves as belonging to the Benedictine order until 1610.[12] The first Lutheran pastor was sent to Wienhausen in 1529, and the Duke of Brunswick later took away much of the convent's land and all its prayer books. Church services were not switched from Latin to German until 1602, however, and until the 1640s residents who died provided in their wills for candles to be lit perpetually for the repose of their souls. The first woman willingly left the convent to marry only in 1651.[13] Evidence from convents in Brunswick and Augsburg indicates that Protestant and Catholic women lived together quite peacefully for decades, protected by the walls of their convent from the religious conflicts surrounding them. The distinction between Protestant and Catholic that is so important in understanding the religious and intellectual history of sixteenth-century Europe may

have ultimately been less important to the women who lived in convents or other religious institutions than the distinction between their pattern of life and that of the majority of laywomen.

Anna Sophia's writings point out that conflict over women's life in convents did not end with the period of the Reformation, nor even with the hardening of religious divisions after the Thirty Years War. The final source in this volume comes from a woman who lived in and then left a different sort of religious establishment, one which followed neither any of the Catholic rules existing prior to the Reformation nor the Augsburg Confession. Like Ursula of Münsterberg, Martha Elisabeth Zitter also left a Catholic convent, but one that was part of a new religious order, the Ursulines, founded in the sixteenth century as part of the Catholic Reformation.

One of the key parts of the Catholic response to the Protestant Reformation was the founding of new religious orders, of which the Society of Jesus, the Jesuits, was the most important. Women who wanted to form female counterparts to the Jesuits ran into trouble with church authorities, however, for another central aim of the Catholic Reformation was an enforcement of cloistering for women. Reforms of the church beginning with the Gregorian in the eleventh century had all emphasized the importance of the control of female sexuality and the inappropriateness of women religious being in contact with lay society; claustration was a key part of the restrictions on Beguines in the fourteenth century and of the fifteenth-century reform of the convents. The problem became even more acute after the Protestant Reformation, for numerous women in Europe felt God had called them to oppose Protestants directly through missionary work, or to carry out the type of active service to the world in schools and hospitals that the Franciscans, Dominicans, and the new orders like the Jesuits were making increasingly popular with men.

The Company of St. Ursula, or Ursulines, was founded in Brescia, Italy by just such a woman, Angela Merici. The Company was a group of lay single women and widows dedicated to serving the poor, the ill, orphans, and war victims, earning their own living through teaching or weaving. Merici received papal approval in 1535, for the Pope saw this as a counterpart to the large number of men's lay confraternities and societies that were springing up in Italy as part of the movement to reform the church.

Similar groups of laywomen dedicated to charitable service began to spring up in other cities of Italy, Spain, and France, and in 1541, Isabel Roser decided to go one step further and ask for papal approval for an order of religious women with a similar mission. Roser had been an associate of Ignatius Loyola, the founder of the Jesuits, in Barcelona. She saw her group as a female order of Jesuits which, like the Jesuits, would not be cut off from the world but would devote itself to education, care of the sick, and assistance to the poor, and in so doing win converts back to Catholicism. This was going too far, however. Loyola was horrified at the thought of religious women in constant contact with lay people and Pope Paul III refused to grant his approval. Despite this, her group continued to grow in Rome and in the Netherlands, where they spread Loyola's teaching through the use of the Jesuit catechism.

The Council of Trent, the church council which met in 1545-1563 to define what Catholic positions would be on matters of doctrine and discipline, reaffirmed the necessity of cloister for all women religious and called for an end to open monasteries and other uncloistered communities such as canoness houses. Enforcement of this decree came slowly, however, for several reasons. First, women's communities themselves fought it or ignored it. Followers of Isabel Roser, for example, were still active into the seventeenth century, for in 1630 Pope Urban VIII published a Bull to suppress them, and reported that they were building convents and choosing abbesses and rectors. The residents of some of Roser's communities and other convents which fought strict claustration were often from wealthy urban families who could pressure church officials. Second, church officials themselves recognized the value of the services performed by such communities, particularly in the area of girls' education and care of the sick. Well after Trent, Charles Borromeo, a reforming archbishop in Milan, invited in members of the Company of St. Ursula, and transformed the group from one of laywomen into one of religious who lived communally, though they still were not cloistered. From Milan, the Ursulines spread throughout the rest of Italy and into France and began to focus completely on the education of girls. They became so popular that noble families began to send their daughters to Ursuline houses for an education, and girls from wealthy families became Ursulines themselves.

The very success of the Ursulines led to the enforcement of claustration, however, as well as other Tridentine decrees regulating women religious. Wealthy families were uncomfortable with the fact that because Ursulines did not take solemn vows, their daughters who had joined communities could theoretically leave at any time and make a claim on family inheritance. They thus took the opposite position to noble families in the Middle Ages, who had generally supported open religious communities for women such as the canoness houses because of the flexibility it gave them in using their daughters for marriage alliances. Gradually the Ursuline houses in France and Italy were ordered to accept claustration, take solemn vows, and put themselves under the authority of their local bishop, thus preventing any movement or cooperation between houses. They were still allowed to teach girls, but now only within the confines of a convent. Some houses fought this as long as they could, though others accepted claustration willingly, having fully internalized church teachings that the life of a cloistered nun was the most worthy in the eyes of God.[14]

The Ursulines were slower in coming into Germany than France, with the first affiliated group, a company of women similar to Merici's original group in Brescia, founded in Cologne in 1606. This Company of St. Ursula (*Gesellschaft der heilige Ursula*) was originally not a religious house, but a group of laywomen who devoted themselves to serving the poor.[15] Many of those who joined quickly came to think of themselves as religious, though they took no vows, and a rule was drawn up to guide them which closely followed the rules of Ursuline convents elsewhere. They began to wear habits and modeled themselves on the Jesuits, claiming obedience to no other authority than the pope. Along with women elsewhere in Europe, they were attempting to create a middle position between lay and religious, and were somewhat successful in Cologne, though their model did not spread in Germany. The Ursuline groups that were more successful were those which followed the French model, opening cloistered communities for women which concentrated on educating girls. It is this type of Ursuline community that Martha Zimmer decided to leave, a community which she, in fact, calls the "French Ursuline Order."

Along with new types of religious orders, the seventeenth century brought other changes to convent life. During the middle of the Thirty

Years War, the emperor issued the Edict of Restitution, ordering all territories, including convents, which had become Protestant after 1555 to return to Catholicism. Protestant convents and canoness houses fought this in the same way that they had earlier fought Protestantism, pressuring local nobles to assist them and refusing to allow Catholic preachers within their walls.[16] Those who were forced to accept the change attempted to retain as many of their traditions as they could. When with the Edict of Restitution Heiningen was returned to Catholicism, for example, the Jesuits wanted to take over part of the convent's income, but the nuns adamantly refused. The Jesuits tried again by sending two representatives, but the nuns would not let them in the door.[17]

Thus despite convent walls, the experience of women religious in the sixteenth and seventeenth centuries is not separate from the general history of the period, in the same way that women's history in any period is not separate from that of men. Their experience was not the same as that of laywomen, of course, and they were further separated from most women of the time by the fact that they were literate and have left us a historical record of their thoughts. We must use this historical record — the sources translated here — carefully, for, except for Anna Sophia's book of meditations, they were originally printed not because the authors themselves thought them important, but because they could be used in the religious controversies of early modern Germany. We have no way of knowing how editors and publishers — who were men — may have altered the words.

These same reservations apply, of course, to almost all texts from early modern society, by men or women. All of them come from the literate minority, and all may have been edited and changed without the author's knowledge. Even someone as prominent as Martin Luther complained repeatedly that printers were publishing his works without his approval or oversight, introducing changes and errors. Thus as long as we understand that these texts provide us with only part of the picture, we can use them to broaden our understanding of both women's lives and religion in early modern society.

Notes

1. Roland Bainton, *Women of the Reformation in Germany and Italy,*
Women of the Reformation in France and England, and *Women of*
the Reformation from Spain to Scandinavia (Minneapolis: Augsburg
Publishing House, 1971, 1973, 1977).
2. Katherine von Bora appears to have left no extant writings, though
there are references in other sources to her letters. There are no
recent biographies of her in English, though there is a popular
biography of Luther which includes discussion of her: Dolina
MacCuish,*Luther and His Katie* (Fearn, Tain, Ross-Shire, Scot-
land: Christian Focus Publications, 1993). There are several recent biographies in German, including: Martin Treu, *Katherina*
von Bora, Biographien zur Reformation (Wittenberg: Drei
Kastanien Verlag, 1995); Ursula Sachau, *Das Letzte Geheimnis:*
Das Leben und die Zeit der Katherine von Bora (Munich: Ehren
Wirth, 1991); Ingelore Winter, *Katherina von Bora: Ein Leben*
mit Martin Luther (Dusseldorf: Droste, 1990). Jeannette C. Smith
is currently preparing an annotated bibliography of all available
works, entitled "Katherine von Bora Luther: A Bibliography." My
thanks to her for the above references.
3. The writings of Charitas Pirckheimer have been reprinted in German in modern editions by Josef Pfanner: *Das "Gebetbuch" der*
Charitas Pirckheimer (Landshut: Solanus, 1962); *Die "Denck-*
würdigkeiten" der Charitas Pirckheimer (Landshut: Solanus,
1962); *Briefe von, an und über Charitas Pirckheimer* (Landshut:
Solanus, 1962). Selections from these have been translated into
English in Gwendolyn Bryant, "The Nuremberg Abbess: Charitas
Pirckheimer," in Katharina M. Wilson, ed., *Women Writers of*
the Renaissance and Reformation, (Athens: University of Georgia
Press, 1987), 287-303. The quotation is from pages 298 and 300.
4. Quoted in Franz Schrader, *Ringen, Untergang und Überleben der*
Katholischen Klöster in den Hochstiften Magdeburg und Halberstadt
von der Reformation bis zum Westphalischen Frieden, Katholisches
Leben und Kirchenreform im Zeitalter der Glaubensspaltung, vol.
37 (Münster: Aschendorff, 1977), 74. The same gender difference was found in France during the Revolution, when nuns were
much more likely than monks to stay in their communities. (Olwen

Hufton and Frank Tallett, "Communities of Women, the Religious Life, and Public Service in Eighteenth-Century France," in Marilyn Boxer and Jean Quataert , eds., *Connecting Spheres: Women in the Western World, 1500 to the Present* [New York: Oxford University Press, 1987], 76.)

5. Adolph Wrede, *Die Einführung der Reformation im Lünebergischen durch Herzog Ernst den Bekenner* (Göttingen: Dietrich, 1887), 127, 217.

6. Ulrich Faust, ed., *Die* Frauenklöster *in Niedersachsen, Schleswig-Holstein und Bremen*, Germania Benedictina, vol. 11: Norddeutschland (St. Ottilien: EOS-Verlag, 1984), 384.

7. Gerhard Taddy, *Das Kloster Heiningen von der Gründung bis zur Aufhebung*, Veröffentlichung des Max-Planck Instituts für Geschichte, 14 (Göttingen: Vandenhoeck und Ruprecht, 1966), 120, 122.

8. Schrader, *Ringen*, 43.

9. Quoted in Johann Karl Seidemann, *Dr. Jacob Schenk, der vermeintlicher Antinomer, Freibergs Reformator* (Leipzig: C. Hinrichs'sche, 1875), Anhang 7, 193.

10. "Wittenberger Artikel, 1536," *Quellenschriften zur Geschichte des Protestantismus* 2 (Leipzig: A. Deichert, 1905), 75.

11. Friedrich Ernst Kettner, *Kirchen und Reformations Historie des Kayserl. Freyen Weltichen Stiffts Quedlinburg* (Quedlinburg: Theodore Schwan, 1710), 130.

12. Faust, *Frauenklöster*, 385.

13. *Chronik und Totenbuch des Klosters Wienhausen* (Wienhausen: Kloster Wienhausen, 1986), fols. 70, 82, 88, 89.

14. Elizabeth Rapley, *The Dévotes: Women and Church in Seventeenth-Century Europe* (Montreal and Kingston: McGill/Queen's University Press, 1990).

15. Anne Conrad, *Zwischen Kloster und Welt: Ursulinen und Jesuitinnen in der Katholischen Reformbewegung des 16./17. Jahrhunderts* (Mainz: Philipp von Zabern, 1991).

16. Lucia Koch, "Vom Kloster zum protestantischen Damenstift: Die Nassauischen Stifte Gnadenthal und Walsdorf in der 2. Hälfte des 16. Jahrhunderts" (MA Thesis, University of Mainz, 1995).

17. Taddy, *Kloster Heiningen*, 184.

Bibliography

Because this is a relatively new field of study, there are not many works available in either German or English. In addition to those listed in the notes, you may wish to consult the following:

Braun, Ute. "Hochadelige Frauen des kaiserlich-freiweltlichen Damenstifts Essen: Neue Fragestellung." In *Vergessene Frauen an der Ruhr: Von Herscherinnen und Hörigen, Hausfrauen und Hexen 800-1800*, edited by Bea Lundt., 51-75. Cologne: Böhlau, 1992. 51-75.

Heutger, Nicolaus. *Evangelische Konvente in den welfischen Landen und der Grafschaft Schaumburg: Studien über ein Nachleben klösterlicher und stiftischer Former seit Einführung der Reformation.* Hildesheim: 1981.

Marshall, Sherrin, ed. *Women in Reformation and Counter-Reformation Europe.* Indianapolis and Bloomington: University of Indiana Press, 1989.

McNamara, JoAnn. *Sisters In Arms: A History of Catholic Nuns over Two Millenia.* Cambridge: Harvard University Press, 1996.

Norberg, Kathryn. "The Counter-Reformation and Women Religious and Lay." In *Catholicism in Early Modern History: A Guide to Research,* edited by John O'Malley, S.J.,133-146. St. Louis: Center for Reformation Research, 1988.

Nowicki-Pastuschka, Angelika. *Frauen in der Reformation: Untersuchungen zum Verhalten von Frauen in den Reichstädten Augsburg und Nürnberg zur reformatorischen Bewegung zwischen 1517 und 1537.* Pfaffenweiler: Centaurus, 1990.

Paulus, N. "Glaubenstreue der Lüneberger Klosterfrauen im 16. Jahrhundert," *Historische-politische Blätter* 112 (1893): 635-649.

Roper, Lyndal. *The Holy Household: Women and Morals in Reformation Augsburg.* Oxford: Oxford University Press, 1989.

Wiesner, Merry E. "Ideology Meets the Empire: Reformed Convents and the Reformation." In *Germania Illustrata: Essays on Early Modern Germany Presented to Gerald Strauss,* edited by Andrew C. Fix and Susan C. Karant-Nunn, 181-195. Kirksville, Missouri: Sixteenth Century Essays and Studies, 1992.

Wunder, Heide. *"Er ist die Sonn', sie ist der Mond": Frauen in der Frühen Neuzeit* . Munich: Beck, 1992.

Katherine Rem

Antwurt zwayer Closter frauwen im Katheriner Closter zu Augspurg an Bernhart Remen Und hernach seyn gegen Antwurt.

Katherine Rem

The answer of two nuns in the Katherine Convent of Augsburg to Bernhart Rem and afterwards his answer to this.

Katherine Rem

Antwurt zwayer Closter frauwen im Katheriner Closter zu Augspurg
an Bernhart Remen Und hernach seyn gegen Antwurt.

Esaie. xxxiii.
Gott ist unser gesatz geber.

Job. viii.
Die hoffnung ains gleyßners zergat.

Mein bruder Bernhart,
    du haßt unns gewünscht die rechte erkantnus Jhesu Christi, darumb
wir dir dancken, wir hoffen, wir haben die rechten erkantnuß von
got. Got will uns festen und bestetten, in dem das im von uns ain lob
und ain gefallen ist. Du hast uns zwen Sendbrieff geschickt, schick
ich dir wider. Wann wir achten dich für der falschen Propheten ainen
darvor uns Jesu Christi gewarnet im hayligen Ewangelio. Da er spricht,
Hüttend euch vor den Propheten, die da kommen in gestalt der
scheflach und seind reyssent wölff. Also bist du auch kommen mit vil
gutten worten, und woltest uns gern verirren und klainmütig machen.
Du darfft nit gedencken, das wir so thoret seyen, das wir unser
hoffnung ins Closter und in unser werck setzen, sunder in got setzen
wir unser hofnung. Der ist der recht herr und beloner aller ding, dem
wol wir gern willigklichen im closter dienen lieber dann in der welt,
mit der gnad und hilff gottes. Du darffst dich gantz nichts kümmern
umb unser leib und sel, du darfst für uns nit gen himel noch gen hell
faren, got der almechtig wirt uns alle richten an dem jungsten tag,
nach seiner gerechtigkait, das wiß wir alle wol. Darumb gedenck nu
an dich selb, das du ain gutter Christ werdest und seyest, and das du
dein stand recht haltest, and du bey Gottes namen und bey seiner
bittern marter nit also schwerest. Ich waiß wol das dus wol kanst.
Und am Freytag und Samstag nit flaysch essest. Die ding seynd nit
die leer Jesu Christi, du wilt uns ain agen auß dem aug ziehen, unnd
du hast selb ain grossen thraum darynn. Ich wayß auch wol, das du
gesprochen hast, dein dochter und ich weren dir gleych als mer in
dem Tempel hauß als in der closter. Du soltest dich in dein hertz
hinein schemen, zu gedencken, geschweygen auß zu sprechen. Wers
von dir hört, kan nit vil gutts gedencken über dich. Da sehen wir wol

Katherine Rem

The answer of two nuns in the Katherine Convent of Augsburg to Bernhart Rem and afterwards his answer to this.

Isaiah 33
God is our law giver.

Job 8
The hope of a hypocrite melts away.

My brother Bernhart,

You have wished us the correct understanding of Jesus Christ. We thank you for that. We hope we have the correct understanding of God. God will fortify us because we praise and favor him. You have sent us two letters, which I am returning to you. We regard you as one of the false prophets that Jesus warned us against in the Holy Gospels when he said "Guard yourselves against prophets who come in the form of a sheep and are ravening wolves." Therefore you have also come with many good words and wanted to lead us astray and make us despondent. You should not think that we are so foolish that we place our hope in the convent and in our own works. Rather we place our hope in God. He is the true lord and rewarder of all things. Him do we serve more willingly in the convent than in the world, with the grace and help of God. You do not have to worry at all about our bodies and souls. You do not have to go to heaven or hell for us. God the Almighty will judge all of us at the Last Judgment, according to his justice. We all know that for certain. Therefore think about yourself, that you will become and be a good Christian and that you keep to your station in life rightly and that you do not swear by God's name and by his bitter martyrs. I know that you certainly can do this, and not eat meat on Friday or Saturday. These things are not the teachings of Jesus Christ. You will pull a splinter out of our eye, while you yourself have a large log in yours. I certainly know that you have said that your daughter and I are to you more as if we were in a brothel[1] than in a convent. You should shame yourself in your heart to think [such a thing] to say nothing of saying this. Whoever hears this from you cannot think very well of you. There we certainly see

dein brüderliche lieb, die du zu uns hast und das du von uns last trucken, der Buchtrucker gedenckt freylich nit vil guts über dich. Wenn er dir schon gute wort gibt, hastu nichts anders kinden drucken, wenn von den gaystlichen was sy thund und seyndt. Du hettest das gelt wol durch gots willen geben, warumb hastu nit von dir selbs lassen drucken und deins gleychen. Aber ich wayß wol, das du und deins gleychen recht thund alweg, und das ir die gaystlichen gnug außrichtend, es leyt nichts daran. Es wirdt noch ain zeyt kommen, es würdt euch layd. Wir wöllens mitt der hilff Gotes gern leyden von seindtwegen, er hatt auch bitterlich von unser wegen gelitten. Vergeb euchs got allen, das sey unser böse red, das bitter leyden Jhesu Christi druck in dein hertz, ist dir besser wenn das hin und her gryblen. Du bist nu gern ain gutter gesell unnd frölich. Ich wölt dir dein Sendbrieff wol bas verantwurten, ich wils aber gott dem herren entpfelhen. Du hast uns empotten, du wöllest schier zu uns kommen, wenn du nit von gutter fraindtschafft zu uns kumpst, so bleyb nu auß. Wilt du uns nun außrichten, so dürff wir dein gantz nichts, du darfst uns nichts sollichs mer schicken, wir werdens nit annemen. Wir haben auch gutten bücher vil.

Hernach volget die antwurt auff disen brieff.

Bernhart Rem wünscht seiner Schwester Katherina und Dochter Veronica Remyn frid und Gnad in Christo.

Ich hab ewer antwurt empfangen, aber mit weniger frewd, angesehen das ir mein schreyben in aller Christlicher trew gethon verschmecht und mir mit unwillen mein vermanung wider zu hauß geschickt, darzu auß zorn des ich mich zu euch kains wegs hett versehen, mich schmehen und ain falschen propheten nennen. Zu wölchen worten ich nicht hörters sag, dann das ir noch nit wist, oder nit wissen wölt, was ain falscher Prophet sey. Dann ain falscher prophet braucht wol gute wort zu betrug der ainfeltigen hertzen, die er mit seyn selbs trömen und menschen leer (Hiere. 23) arglistigklich ab zeücht von der haylsamen leer Christi jesu, deren ich (also ist mir got ain zeug) kains gethon hab (Timo. 4) sunder ainfaltigklich auß Christlicher trew euch fürgehalten als vor augen nit menschen leer die verwirren, sonder gotes leer zu gaystlichen frid und frewd ewer gewissen. Menschen leer zerstört und verwirt die hertzen und zeucht sy ab von der warhaftigen

the brotherly love that you have for us. And that you allowed [the letter] from us to be printed![2] The printer certainly does not think very well of you, even if he asked you with good words, "Don't you have anything else to be printed about the religious [orders], what they are doing and how they are?" You should have given [up] the money through God's will. Why didn't you have [things written] by you and others like you printed? But I certainly know that you and those like you always do the right thing, and that the religious [orders] delivered enough to you. No one is sorry for this. There will still come a time when you will suffer. We will gladly suffer for God's sake with the help of God. He has also suffered greatly for our sake. God forgive you for everything. That is our angry message, [that] the bitter suffering of Jesus Christ press in your heart. It would be better for you if you mulled this over. You are a good fellow and happy. I wanted to answer your letter more fully, but I will commend it to God the Lord. You have shocked us because you actually wanted to come to us. If you don't come in kinship, stay out. If you want to straighten us out, then we don't want your [message] at all. You may not send us such things any more. We will not accept them. We also [already] have many good books.

Here follows the answer to this letter.

Bernhart Rem wishes his sister Katherine and daughter Veronica Rem peace and grace in Christ.

I have received your answer but have viewed with little pleasure [the fact] that you have scorned my letter, written in all Christian faith, and that you have sent my admonition back to my house, and this in anger, that I certainly did not anticipate. [You] insulted me and called me a false prophet. To these words I will say nothing harder than that you do not yet know or do not want to know, what a false prophet is. For a false prophet uses fine words to deceive simple hearts, which he cunningly separates from the healing words of Jesus Christ with his own illusions and human teaching. This I have — God is my witness — never done, but simply out of Christian faith, held before you not human teaching which confuses, but God's teaching, for your spiritual peace and the pleasure of your conscience. Human teaching destroys and confuses the heart, and pulls one away from the true and

ainfeltigen leer Christi unsers haylands ii. Cor. xi. gleich wie der
schlang Evam betrog durch sein arglistigkait. Mein schreiben an euch
gethon ist allenthalb offenbar, ich acht auch es müg kein rechter
christ solchs mit grund verwerffen. Aber ir seind mit ewer Regel und
menschen sündlein noch ubel verstrickt, das ir die augenscheinlich
Evangelisch warhait nit mügen fassen. Ich bitt aber Christus, er wöll
ewer hertz erleychten in rechter erkantnuß seiner theüren freyhait,
die er uns so hart, durch ain ellen den verschmechten todt erarbait
hat. Ich hab das mein gethon, als ewer bruder in Christo. Ich kan
euch die gnad nitt geben, aber so vil an mir ist, hab ich treüwe
ermanung gethon, die reüt mich noch nit, wie wol ir in bitterkait
ewers hertzen gegen mir erzünt seyt. Ir schreybt ewer hoffnung stand
allain in got das hör ich gern, und bitt got, das er solliche hoffnung
in euch mere. Das aber ir got gern willigklich im Closter dienen
wölt, fürcht ich es stand die sach umm euch noch nit so glat, als irs
machend, dann ich euch auß Esa. xxix. und Math. 15 gnugsamlich
bericht hab, wie got nit wöl geert werden mit menschen leer und
satzung als ich besorg, das ir noch auff dem alten weg seyt, und mit
selbs erdachten wercken got übel erzürnt, die edelen zeyt schedlich
verzeret, und euch selbs on frucht der lieb auch on lust unnd frewd
der gewissen fast ser bemüet, darzu wölt ir nit verston was welt hayst.
Warlich die weyl wir in der gebrechlichen herberg unsers tödtlichen
leybs wonen, tragen wir die welt alweg mit uns, in welden, in clöstern,
und wa wir seyen. Was beklagt sich sunst Paulus so hart, als seines
sterplichen sündtlichen leybs, darinn sich die erbsünd gwaltigklich
erhept, und streyt wider den gayst gottes in uns tag und nacht, im
Closter und ausserthalb dem Closter, als ir habt Roma. vii. Gal. v.
Darumb secht euch für, seyt nicht schlafferig und sicher hinder den
hohen mauren. Ir seyt warlich in der welt und ob ir schon ettwo nit so vil
args sehend als ich, so habt ir doch bey und in euch selbs die sünd unnd
der sünde frücht. Dann ir seyt nit hailiger dann Paulus der sich sollichs
auch beklagt hatt zu meermal. Es laut nit wol ewer schreyben an
dem ort, es stünd dem gleyßner baß an. Luce xviii. Der nit was wie die
andern, auch begert ir, ich sol mich weder umb ewer leyb noch seel fast
kümmern, ich müß für euch weder gen hymel noch gen hell. Hie merck
ich aber, das ir layder noch nit wist was ain Christlichs leben ist und was
ains Christen menschen ampt ist, dann ir vermaint es soll sich
nyemands des andern annemen und yeder man sein selbs allain gewar
nemen, wa bleybt dann Christlich trew und liebe, die all gebot erfüllt.

simply teachings of Christ our Savior (2 Cor. 11), just like the snake deceived Eve through its cunning. My letter to you is clear in all things. I also notice that no true Christian could have rejected it with cause. But you are still badly ensnared in your rule and human sins, so that you cannot grasp the self-evident evangelical truth. I therefore pray to Christ [that] he will enlighten your hearts to the true understanding of his costly freedom, that he earned for us through a hard and scornful death. I have done this as your brother in Christ. I cannot give you grace, but so much is on me [that] I have given you a true warning. I do not repent this even though you are now enraged against me in the bitterness of your hearts. You write that your hope stands alone in God. I am glad to hear that and ask God that he increase such hope in you. However, that you [say you] want to serve God willingly in the convent, makes me fear that things will not go as smoothly with you as you say, for I have given you enough reports from Isaiah 29 and Matthew 15 that God does not want to be honored with human teachings and laws. I am concerned that you are still on the old path and [that you] make God very angry with works that you have thought up yourselves, that precious time is consumed in a destructive way, and that you are very troubled without joy and happiness in your conscience, and also without the fruits of love, and that you do not want to understand what "the world" means. Truly, because we live in the weak shelter of our mortal bodies, we always carry the world with us, in the fields, in the convents, and wherever we are. What did Saint Paul complain about as much as his mortal, sinful body, in which original sin raised itself so strongly and fought against the spirit of God day and night, in the convent and outside of the convent, as you have in Romans 7 [and] Galatians 5. Be on guard not to be sleepy and too secure behind high walls. You are truly in the world, and if you don't yet see as much wickedness as I do, so you still have sin and the fruits of sin near and in yourselves. For you are not holier than Paul who complained about this in himself many times. This part of your letter does not sound good; it suits the hypocrite well who was not like the others (Luke 18). You also desire that I do not bother myself about your body or soul, or [go to] heaven or hell for you. Here I notice that unfortunately you don't yet know what a Christian life is and what a Christian person's duties are. For you suppose that no one should take on anyone else, and everyone take on only themselves. Where then is Christian faith and love,

Ro. xiii. Bin ich doch schuldig auß gotes gebot euch als meinen neben
menschen zu warnen und zu gutem emanen, ob ir mir schon nit
leyplich gefraint werend, als ir leßt Mat. xviii...
Zu letst begebt ir euch willigklich in durchechtung, gleich als ob es
ain durchechtung hayß wenn man euch mit schrift fraintlich ermant.
O wölt ir dem leyden christi gleichförmig werden, so müst ir anders
leyden. Seyt ir nit in der welt, warumb beyssen euch denn die wort
gotes so ubel, so sy ewer leben ain wenig antasten. Ich wölt ir hetten
alle kunst brauch auf mein brief wol zu antwurten, ir antwurt aber
nu zornige wortes lat sich die lauttern schrifft nitt so leychtlich
verantwurten. Nempt all ewere bücher und gebt grundtliche antwurt,
seyt ir so gelert. Ir wölt auch kain schrifft oder ermanung mer von
mir annemen, da sich ich aber das ir zornig seyt, wer zorn und neyd
hat, der ist noch in der welt. Ir habt zorn in euch, darumb seyt ir der
wellt noch nit ertrunnen. Das ir aber vil bücher habt, gib ich zu, aber
ich bit euch, leßt das einig buch die Bibel mit fleyß und gotsforcht,
und lond die andern vil bücher faren, so werdt ir darnach wol sehen,
auß was grund ich euch zu geschryben hab, und mich kain falschen
propheten mer nennen. Ir wert ewer selbs gelassenhait lernen, aygen
guttbeduncken faren lassen, und auch des aller grösten sünders sorg
und gebet für euch nit verachten wie ir mir thon habt, wolan ich will
euchs als zu gut nemen. Zu beschluß, zürnet, aber sündet nit, laßt
die sunnen nit uber ewern zorn nider gon. Psal. iiii. Ephe. iiii. Und
laßt euch ain sünder und flaischlichen auß christlicher trew ains gesagt
haben. Es sey denn das ir ewer leben nach dem wort gotts richten,
das allain unser liecht und Regel ist götlich zu leben und menschen
leer lassen ligen. So will ich lieber mitt dem offen sünder im tempel.
Luce. xviii. flaischlich genennt werden, dann mit euch und ewers
gleichen gaystlich sein. Darbey wünsch ich euch aber ain mal rechte
erkantnuß Jhesu Christi, dz der gayst der lebendig macht, in ewer
hertz schreyb, die uberschwencklich gutthet Christi, das ir wyst
warumb er in menschlicher natur anß Creütz gehefft sey. Wann ir das
wist, so wer den menschen findlein und vertraw auff aygne werck, kutten,
Closter, speyß meyden, und der gleych gar bald abfallen. Es will gar
ernstlich auffsehen haben, das man hie sich nit vermeß mit gaystlicher
Symoney die Gottes gnad zu kauffen, wer oren hab zu hören der hör. Es
ist gar ain haimlich laster, tyeff in unser sündige natur eingewurtzelt.
Solliche vermessenhait, die alweg vermaynt gott fürzukommen, und durch
ire aygne werck ain gnedigen got zu machen, es mag sich der mensch

that fulfills all commandments (Rom. 13)? I am nevertheless responsible, according to God's commandments, to warn you and give you good advice as my fellow human beings, even if you were not related to me (Matt. 18). . . .

Lastly, expose yourselves willingly to slander, just as if it might be called slander when one admonishes you in a friendly way in writing. Oh, if you want to become like the suffering Christ, you must suffer in a different way. If you are not in the world, why does the Word of God sting you so badly, making you question your life a bit? I wish you had used all the arts to answer my letter. You answer only the angry words; the letter itself is not so easy to answer. Take all your books and give basic answers if you are so learned. You don't want to accept any writings or admonitions from me. In this I see that you are angry. Whoever has anger and envy is still in the world. You have anger in you; therefore you have not yet escaped the world. I admit, however, that you have many books, but I request that you read only the Bible with diligence and fear of God, and let the other books go. Then you will certainly see, for what reasons I have written to you and [you] won't call me a false prophet anymore. You will learn composure and let your vanity go, and also not despise the worries and prayers for you [which come from] the worst sinner, as you have done to me, even though I wanted to do this for your benefit. In conclusion, be angry, but do not sin; do not let the sun go down on your anger (Ps. 4, Eph. 4). And let a sinner and mortal say one thing to you out of Christian faith: This is that you arrange your life according to the Word of God, which is our only light and rule. Live in a godly manner and let human teachings lie. I would rather be counted as carnal with the open sinners in the temple (Luke 18) than be religious with you and those like you. Nevertheless I wish you for once the correct knowledge of Jesus Christ, that the spirit that brings life would write in your hearts the overflowing good works of Christ, so that you know why he in human nature was fastened to the cross. When you know that, your little human discoveries and trust in your own works, habits, convent, fasting, and such things will soon fall away. It will be looked upon as very serious, for one does not presume to buy God's grace with spiritual simony. Who has ears to hear, let them hear. It is a secret vice rooted deep in our sinful nature. Such presumption, that always presumes one is more facile than God and can achieve God's grace through one's own work. It might be that a

herauß mit müe solches gotloßen yrsals erweren, will geschweigen in
Clöstern, da vil und mancherlay selbs erwölte werck mit feynen glantz
der hailigkait geyebt werden, und ist als Auen und Amal, man mach
darauß was man wöll. Aber leßet mitt ernstlichem auffmercken den
v. und xiii. Psalmen wie in Paulus Roman. iii. einfiert auff das ir
dester leychter mügt menschen werck erkennen. Die gnad Gottes
sey mitt euch allen. Amen. Datum Freytags den Aylfften tag
Septembris. Im M.D.xxiii. Jar in Augspurg.

person could, with effort, ward off such godless error, but I will say nothing about the convents, where many different types of work — all of it self-chosen — are practiced with the fine glitter of holiness. And it is worthless straw, whatever one makes of it. But read with serious attention the 5th and 13th Psalms as Paul inserts [them] in Romans 3, so that you can recognize human works more easily. The grace of God be with you all. Amen. Date: Friday, September 11, 1523 in Augsburg.

Notes

1. The words Katherine Rem actually uses here are "Tempel haus," a reference to what is often called "temple prostitution" in the ancient Near East. In some religious traditions that were contemporaneous with the ancient Hebrews, the sexual services of temple personnel — priests and priestesses — were considered part of their priestly functions for specific festivals and holidays.
2. Bernhard Rem had already given an earlier letter from his sister to a printer for publication, along with his answer, and had also published two of his earlier letters to them. This is at a point in the early Reformation when pamphlets of religious controversy sold very well, which explains Katherine Rem's statement about money in the next sentence.

Ursula of Münsterberg

Der Durchlauchtigen Hochgebornen F(rau) Ursulen, Herzogin zu Münsterberg u., Gräfin zu Glatz u., christliche Ursach des verlassenen Klosters zu Freiberg.

Ursula of Münsterberg

The enlightened and highborn Lady Ursula, Countess of Münsterberg, etc., Duchess of Glatz, etc., [gives] Christian reasons for abandoning the convent of Freiberg.

Ursula of Münsterberg

Der Durchlauchtigen Hochgebornen F(rau) Ursulen, Herzogin zu
Münsterberg u., Gräfin zu Glatz u., christliche Ursach des verlassenen
Klosters zu Freiberg.

Den Hochgebornen Fürsten und Herren, Herrn Georgen und
Herrn Heinrichen, Herzogen zu Sachsen, Landgrafen in Thüringen,
Markgrafen zu Meißen, meinen freundlichen lieben Herren und
Ohmen.

1. Gnade und Friede in Christo, unserm Heiland, zuvor,
hochgeborne Fürsten, freundliche liebe Herren und Ohme. Nachdem
ich verständigt, daß euer Lieben beiderseits merklichen Ungefallen
tragen derhalben, daß ich sammt zween Jungfrauen mich aus dem
Kloster zu Freiberg begeben und meinen Orden verlassen habe, aus
welchem sich E.L. vermuthen, es geschehe ein solches aus
leichtfertigem Vorwitz:
2. Auf das habe ich E.L. mein Gemüthe und Wohlbedencken nicht
wollen bergen und diese Schrift, so ich mit eigener Hand, aus meinem
Herzen, ohne Hülfe, Rath oder Zuthun irgend eines Menschen auf
Erden geschrieben habe, eben zu dieser Zeit, laut des Dato, so E.L.
hierinnen befinden werden, wollen zugeschrieben, aus welcher E.L.
befinden werden, daß solches aus keiner Leichtfertigkeit geschehen
sei, sondern dieweil ich schuldig bin, vor GOttes Gericht Rechenschaft
zu geben für meine Seele, und bin deß gewiß, daß weder E.L. noch
keine Creatur unter den Himmel mich vor GOtt entschuldigen kann...

1. Paulus, 1 Cor. 10, 32., sagt: "Seid unanstößig beide den Griechen
und Juden, und der Gemeine GOttes." Diesem nach haben wir nicht
wollen unterlassen, vor einem jeden, so es begehrt zu wissen, an Tag
zu geben Grund und Ursachen, durch welche wir verursacht sind,
Klosterleben, sammt denselben Ceremonien, Weisen, Stelle und
Personen zu verlassen, fleißig begehrende, ein jeder frommer Christ,
so solches hören und sehen wird, wollte beherzigen die großen
fährlichen Nöthen unsers Gewissens, darinnen wir gewesen sind, an
welchen er wird befinden, daß wir in keine andern Wege dem
unvermeidlichen Urtheil GOttes, so er dräuet allen Verächtern seines

Ursula of Münsterberg

The enlightened and highborn Lady Ursula, Countess of Münsterberg, etc., Duchess of Glatz, etc., [gives] Christian reasons for abandoning the convent of Freiberg.

To the highborn princes and lords, Lord George and Lord Heinrich, Dukes of Saxony, Landgraves in Thuringia, Margraves of Meissen, my dear friendly lords and cousins.

[Foreword]

1. Grace and peace in Christ our Savior, exalted princes, friendly dear lords and cousins. I have learned that both of your graces have been very uncivil because I have left the convent in Freiberg along with two other women and have left my order. Your graces assume that this happened because of thoughtless impertinence.

2. I do not want to conceal my feelings and deliberations from your graces, and therefore I have written this work with my own hand, out of my own heart, and without the help, advice or contribution of any other person on earth, on the date that you will find within. Through this [work], your graces will discover that this has not happened out of thoughtlessness, but because I am accountable to the judgment of God for my soul, and am sure that neither your graces nor any other creature on earth can excuse me before God. . . .

[Text]

1. Paul (1 Cor. 10:32) says: "Avoid shocking both Greek and Jew and the community of God." For anyone who wishes to know the light, we[1] have not neglected to give the grounds and reasons through which we are motivated to abandon convent life together with its ceremonies, ways of life, position, and persons. Every pious Christian who hears and sees this will take to heart the great and perilous dangers to our conscience. He will find that we could have escaped God's unavoidable judgment — through which he threatens all despisers of

ewigbleibenden wahrhaftigen Wortes, welches er selbst ist, Joh. 1, 1., haben mögen entfliehen, denn eben durch diese Weise.

2. Aus welchen er auch wird erkennen, daß solches aus keinem leichtfertigen Gemüthe geschehen sei, noch aus keinem schnellen Zufall, sondern allenthalben bewogen und wohlbedacht. Sind der Zuversicht zu einem jeden, der durch göttliche Gnade des Glaubens berichtet, und von GOtt gelehrt ist, daß ihm solches kein Aergerniß sein wird, sondern mehr eine Stärkung, GOtt zu loben und preisen, der die Seinen aus solcher fährlicher Noth erretten kann. Wiewohl wir denen, so mit verstockten Herzen GOttes Wort verachten und verfolgen, kein Wort nicht wollen geantwortet haben hierinne, sondern wir lassen sie fahren; denn sie sind blind, welchen Titel ihnen Christus selbst gibt, Matth. 15, 14. Und Joh. 10, 27., sagt er, "daß allein seine Schafe seine Stimme hören." Derhalben, so wir uns allein auf GOtt und sein Wort steuren, wird unsere Verantwortung freilich nichts gelten bei denen, so vor ihren Augen "den gekreuzigten Christum zu einem Aergerniß und Thorheit" haben, welchen wir bekennen "göttliche Kraft und göttliche Weisheit" (1 Cor. 1, 23. 24.), welchem ewiger Preis sei zu ewigen Zeiten, Amen.

3. Die erste Ursache, so uns zwingt, Klosterleben zu verlassen, ist diese: Christus sagt Marci am letzten, V. 15. f.: "Verkündiget das Evangelium allen Creaturen. Wer da glaubt und getauft wird, der wird selig" u., und Joh. 3, 16.: "Also hat GOtt die Welt geliebet, daß er seinen einigen Sohn gab, auf daß alle, die an ihn glauben, nicht verloren werden, sondern das ewige Leben haben" u. Auch der Prophet Habukuk 2, 4. sagt: "Der Gerechte wird seines Glaubens leben." In welchen Sprüchen aufs klärlichste angezeigt ist, daß all unser Heil und Leben blößlich auf Christo stehe, so der im Glauben angenommen wird, wie Joh. 14, 6.: "Ich bin der Weg, die Wahrheit und das Leben, niemand kommt zum Vater, denn durch mich" u...

7. Das erste, so unserm Glauben anstößig und verhinderlich ist, ist das. Dieweil wir nach empfangener Gnade, so in der Taufe uns geschenket, noch müssen streiten und kämpfen mit dem verdammten Fleisch, so durch die erste Geburt verderbt und vergiftet ist durch die Sünde, so fühlen wir auch, daß solcher Kampf schwer und fährlich ist, weil dies Laster so tief in unser Fleisch gewurzelt ist, daß es nicht kann gar ausgerottet werden, so lange dies Fleisch in seinem ersten Wesen bleibt; welches verdammliche Laster ist der Unglaube. Will uns denn nicht gebühren, solch Hinderniß aus dem Wege zu thun,

his everlastingly true Word who he is himself (John 1:1) — in no other way except in this manner.

2. From these things, he will also recognize that this has not happened from a foolhardy disposition nor from hasty spontaneity, but that everything has been considered and well thought out. The confidence is in each one who is informed and taught by God, through the divine grace of faith, that this will not be a stumbling block to him but strengthen him, [allowing him] to love and praise God, who can deliver his own from such dangerous difficulties. We will answer no word in this from those who despise and persecute God's Word with hardened hearts; instead, we let them go because they are blind, a title that Christ himself gives them (Matt. 15:14). And John 10:27 says "that his sheep alone hear his voice." For that reason, because we rely on God and his Word alone, our responsibility will not apply to those who have before their eyes "the crucified Christ as an annoyance and folly," while we acknowledge "the power of God and the wisdom of God" (1 Cor. 1:23-24) whose eternal praise is for eternal ages. Amen.

3. The first reason that persuaded us to leave the convent is this: Christ said in the last chapter of Mark, verse 15f. : "Proclaim the Gospel to all creatures. Who believes and is baptized will be saved," etc., and John 3:16: "God so loved the world that he gave his only son so that all who believe in him will not be lost but have eternal life," etc. The prophet Habakkuk (2:4)also says: "The righteous will live by faith." In these verses it is clearly announced that all our holiness and life stands nakedly in Christ, who will be accepted on faith as in John 14:6: "I am the way, the truth, and the life; no one comes to the Father except through me," etc. . . .

7. The first thing that is shocking and offensive to our faith [in the convent] is this. Because after we receive initial grace in baptism we still must strive and battle with the condemned flesh that is spoiled and poisoned from the first birth through sin, so we also feel that such a fight is difficult and dangerous because this vice is so deeply rooted in our flesh that it cannot truly be cast out as long as this flesh remains in its first state; this damnable vice is unbelief. Is it not our responsibility to put such impediments out of the way in order that we may battle more securely? As reported above, since faith alone

auf daß wir desto sicherer möchten kämpfen? Weil denn nun Glauben allein unsere Seligkeit ist, und Unglauben unsere Verdammniß, wie oben angezeigt, befinden wir dieser Stelle und Ortes ganz das Widerspiel zu sein beides in Worten und Werken, und eben die Gelübde, so sie sagen, unsere Seligkeit solle darinne stehen, die sind es, die uns von GOtte reißen, und werfen uns in Ungewißheit und ewige Verdammniß; derhalben wir sie haben müssen verlassen.

8. Daß wie aber solches verständlicher mögen an Tag geben, so wollen wir GOttes Gebot, unser Taufgelübde, und unsern Tand gegen einander halten, aus welchem ein jeder erkennen kann, wie ferne sie von einander geschieden sind, und wie fährlich der Glaube stehet, und mit welchem Zittern und Beben hierinne stetiglich zu gewarten sei ein schwerer und unwiederbringlicher Fall. Das stellen wir einem jeden gläubigen und versuchten Herzen anheim zu erkennen, wie das bei einander stehen kann, in der Taufe zu geloben, dem Teufel zu entsagen (das ist), sein Reich zu verleugnen (in welches wir durch die erste Geburt verworfen sind) und ewige Feindschaft und Kampf mit ihm zu haben. Und deß zu Urkunde begehren und bitten wir durch das Sacrament der Taufe, angenommen (zu) werden in das Reich Christi (das ist), in die christliche Gemeine, welche, regiert durch das Wort GOttes, sein Eigenthum ist. 1 Petr. 2, 9.

9. Dagegen, was ist doch Häßlichers auch zu gedenken, denn daß wir zu Schmach und Lästerung unsers Königs Christi ein neu Verbündniß machen mit seinem und unserm entsagten Feinde, und schließen uns aus der Gemeinschaft der Kinder GOttes und aus der Brüderschaft Christi und seiner Glieder, eine neue und eigene Brüderschaft zu haben, welche von Menschen erdacht, ohne GOttes Wort und demselben entgegen ist, von welchem der Prophet sagt Ps. 116, 11.: "Ich habe gesagt in meinem Zagen: alle Menschen sind Lügner." So dem denn also, was ist Lügen anders denn Teufelswerk? aus welchem folgt, daß alles, so menschliche Vernunft erdichtet außer GOttes Wort, ist eben dasselbige...

15. Aber wie sollten wir nicht den Geist der Gnaden hiemit geschändet haben, durch den doch allein Vergebung der Sünden geschieht, wie Christus sagt, Joh. 20, 22. 23.? Und noch über das alles, dieweil wir Christo in der Taufe verbunden sind mit unauflöslichem Bande ehelicher Gemahlschaft durch den Glauben, wie Hosea 2, 20.: "Ich habe dich mir vertrauet durch den Glauben." Durch welche Gemahlschaft wir haben empfangen unzählige Güter,

now is our salvation and unbelief our damnation, we find this place and situation [i.e., the convent] wholly the antithesis of it, both in words and works. And even the vows (in which salvation should rest, as they say) throw us who journey to God into uncertainty and eternal damnation; therefore, we had to leave.

8. That we may give light to such understanding, we compare God's command, our baptismal vows, and our trifles to one another, through which everyone can recognize how distantly they are divorced from one another, and how much at risk faith is; to steadily endure in here with such shaking and trembling would be difficult and unrestorable. We put it to all believing and seeking hearts, to recognize internally how they can stand with one another, to vow in baptism to renounce the devil, (that is) to renounce his kingdom (in which we are thrown through the first birth) and to have eternal enmity and war with him. We long to witness to that and pray, through the sacrament of baptism, to be taken into the kingdom of Christ (that is), into the Christian community which, governed through the Word of God, is his possession (1 Pet. 2:9).

9. In contrast, what is more odious to think than that — to the offense and slander of Christ our King — we make a new covenant with his and our renounced enemy, locking ourselves out of the community of the children of God and out of the brotherhood of Christ and his members, in order to have a new and particular brotherhood. This [brotherhood] is fabricated by people without God's Word and contrary to it, about which the prophet says (Ps. 116:11): "I have said in my hesitation: all human beings are liars." So, then, what is a lie other than the work of the devil? From which it follows that everything fabricated from human reason outside of God's Word is the same thing. . . .

15. But how should we not by these actions [i.e., taking vows in the convent] have shamed the Spirit of grace through which alone the forgiveness of sins occurs, as Christ says (John 20:22-23)? And this above all, because we are bound to Christ in baptism with indissoluble bonds of matrimonial spousehood through faith, as in Hosea 2:20: "I have entrusted you to me through faith." Through this spousehood we have received uncountable kindnesses, namely, the merits of Christ gathered from his suffering and death. Through this,

nämlich, die Verdienste Christi, sammt seinem Leiden und Sterben, also daß durch dieselben auch unsere Sünden ganz versenkt sind in dem ungründlichen Brunnen göttlicher Barmherzigkeit, welches wir nicht allein undankbarlich empfangen haben, sondern haben uns auch eine eigene und erdichtete Gemahlschaft zugerichtet, in welcher wir, des Teufels Hoffahrt vollkommen zu machen, mit Ehebrechers Büberei aus der keuschen Ehe Christi getreten sind, nämlich in dem, daß wir neben GOtt, so unser vertrauter Bräutigam durch das Verbündniß des Glaubens, mit einem andern die Ehe verbrechen, nämlich, mit unsern erdichteten Werken, in welche wir vertrauet haben; und haben uns dennoch wohl dürfen rühmen, wir sind Bräute Christi, haben uns noch wohl dazu dürfen überheben über andere Christen, welche wir deß unwürdig geschätzt haben. Welches unsere Worte und Werke klar an Tag geben. Ob es wohl ihrer viel leugnen, wollen es doch wir GOtt zu Lobe nicht schweigen, denn es werden doch solche unsere Sünden vor GOtt und aller Welt bloß und entdeckt erscheinen am Tage des Gerichts. Derhalben wir es besser achten, "daß wir uns selbst richten, auf daß wir nicht gerichtet werden", wie Paulus 1 Cor. 11, 32. sagt.

16. Daß wir aber solche unsere Meinung verständlicher an Tag geben, hat ein jeglicher zu bedenken, so er es anders will zu Herzen fassen, daß diese Gemahlschaft und Verbündniß, so zwischen GOtt und uns gemacht durch den Glauben, so wir öffentlich bekannt haben in der Taufe, verbrochen und beselbet ist in diesem Falle, dieweil wir in der Taufe bekannt haben, und uns verpflichtet zu glauben an den einigen GOtt, in Dreifaltigkeit der Personen. Gehet hie das Verbündniß. Daß es aber verbrochen ist, überzeugt uns GOttes Gesetz im andern Buch Mosis, Cap. 20, 3. 4., da es also spricht: "Du sollst keine andere Götter neben mir haben; du sollst kein Bildniß noch irgend ein Gleichniß machen" u.

17. Wer kann aber hie leugnen, daß es nicht beselbet sei, so wir unserer Hände Werke anbeten und ihnen göttliche Ehre zulegen, und wir ihnen unsere Seligkeit zueignen, welche Ehre allein GOtt zuständig ist, wie oben vermeldet. Und solches haben wir förderlich gethan bei den dreien Gelübden, welche wir bei Verlust der Seelen haben sollen unwandelbar halten. In welchem Falle doch das Gesetz GOttes nicht gelten muß, sondern dem Glauben und der Liebe weichen, wie Matth. 12, 6. 7., Marc. 2, 25. 26., und Luc. 6, 3. 4. Sind sie aber dem Taufgelübde nicht ungemäß und zugegen, so wir hie geloben, keinen

our sins are wholly mediated in the bottomless spring of divine mercy. We have not only received this ungratefully, but we have also contracted a peculiar and fabricated spousehood in which, in order to make the devil's arrogance complete, we have left the chaste marriage of Christ with the knavery of an adulterer. Namely, we have broken our marriage in that along with God, our trusted bridegroom through the bonds of faith, we have allowed ourselves to be glorified as brides of Christ and let ourselves even be lifted up over other Christians who we have regarded as unworthy of this. Our words and works clearly bring this to light. Even if you totally deny it, we would still not keep silent, God be praised, because all our sins will appear naked and revealed before God and the whole world on the day of judgment. For that reason, we regard it better "that we judge ourselves so that we be not judged," as Paul (1 Cor. 11:32) says.

16. So that we make our meaning known more clearly: Each one has to think over — if he will take this to heart in another way — that this spousehood and alliance made between God and us through faith, publicly professed in baptism, is sullied and broken in this case because we have promised and vowed to believe in one God in the Trinity of persons. See the connection here! God's law convinces us that it [i.e., our alliance with God] is broken in the second book of Moses [i.e., Exod.] chapter 20:3-4, where it says: "You shall have no other gods before me; you shall not make images nor any kind of likeness," etc.

17. Who can deny here that it is not of our own [making] when we worship the works of our hands and extend divine honor to them, and when we entrust our salvation to them, though this honor belongs only to God, as was mentioned above? We have done this further with our three vows, to which we would have unchangeably held, to the damage of our souls. In this case, the law of God must not apply, but yield to faith and love as in Matthew 12:6-7, Mark 2:25-26, and Luke 6:3-4. Are they [i.e., the three clerical vows] not opposed to the baptismal vows, which we vowed again here, to have no other gods, to (as mentioned above) renounce the devil, and to bind

andern GOtt zu haben, und, wie oben vermeldet, da wir dem Teufel entsagen, uns verbinden in das Reich GOttes, und allein von ihm im Wort regiert zu werden? 18. Und hie verbinden wir uns zu Gehorsam, aber nicht GOttes, sondern der Menschen, und forthin nicht GOtte, sondern den Menschen zu gehorchen. Welches sich, leider GOttes, tausendfächtig bei uns befunden hat, und im vollen Schwang gangen ist, welches uns unser Gewissen überflüssig überzeugt. Was ist aber das anders, daß wir geloben willig Armuth, welches wir mit dem Munde willig nennen, und mit dem Herzen verleugnen? gerade als wollten wir göttliche Weisheit betrügen als einen Menschen. Es verleugne auch gleich solches, wer da wolle, so bekennen wir doch die Wahrheit. Wir werden es doch vor göttlichem Angesicht nicht bergen können, so er ist "ein Erforscher der Herzen und Begierden." Ps. 7, 10. 19. Darüber, zugegen den Worten Christi, Matth. 5, 3., ist's nicht eine "Armuth des Geistes," sondern nur ein äußerlicher Schein, welcher auch verhinderlich ist, dem Nächsten Liebe und Handreichung zu erzeigen nach dem göttlichen Gesetze. Es wird auch niemand können leugnen, daß die Keuschheit ein Werk sei, das allein GOtt in menschlichem Herzen und Leibe wirken muß; wie sind wir denn so vermessen gewesen, GOtt zu geloben und opfern, das sein, und nicht unser ist? Zuvor, weil wir keinen Befehl von GOtt davon haben, sondern stellen das in eines jeglichen Vermögen, Matth. 19, 12.: "Wer es fassen kann, der fasse es." Sagt aber daselbst kurz davor, V. 11.: "Das Wort fasset nicht jedermann, sondern denen es gegeben ist." Und also alles andere, so diesem Gelübde anhängig ist, als nämlich Regel, Statuten, Constitution, und neue Aufsätze, so ihnen nur einkommen, unter welchen der mehrere Theil GOttes Wort und dem Glauben ungemäß und entgegen ist, aber ja einen Beiweg will haben neben GOtt; welches denn im ersten Gebot aufs stärkste verboten ist, und mit hartem Dräuen des Gesetzes auf das Gewissen dringet. 20. Solches alles würde hie zu lang zu erzählen, derhalben wir es bei dem lassen bleiben; verhoffen, es sei einem jeden Verständigen klar genug an Tag geben, daß er genugsam verstehe, welche Fährlichkeit auf unser Gewissen geladen sei; welche uns in keinen andern Wege ist zu vermeiden gewesen, denn daß wir uns ganz äußerten und "das Unreine nicht mehr anrührten" wie der Prophet Iesaias sagt im 52. Capitel, V. 12...

ourselves to the kingdom of God to be governed by him alone in the Word?

18. And here [i.e., in the convent] we bind ourselves to obedience, but to people rather than God, and [we] henceforth obey not God but people. This is found, most unfortunately, a thousandfold in us, going full swing, with our conscience unnecessarily persuading us. What else is it when we willingly vow poverty, which we willingly speak with our mouths, but deny with our hearts? This is exactly as if we would deceive divine wisdom as human beings. Similarly, it also deceives those who desire that we certainly confess the truth. We cannot conceal it from the divine countenance, because he is "a searcher of the heart and desires" (Ps. 7:10).

19. Moreover, in contrast to the Word of Christ (Matt. 5:3), this is not a "poverty of the Spirit," but only an external appearance, which also hinders one from showing one's fellow human beings love and charity [as one is supposed to] according to divine law. No one can deny that chastity is a quality that God alone can create in human hearts and bodies; how, then, are we so arrogant as to pledge and sacrifice what is God's [to give] and not ours? First, though we have no command from God, [we] set it [i.e., chastity] within everyone's capability (Matt. 19:12): "Whoever can receive it, let him receive it." But the same book says just before this in verse 11: "This precept [i.e., chastity] is not received by everyone, but only those to whom it is granted." And therefore everything else that follows from these vows, that is, rules, statutes, constitutions, and new traditions that come to them, are for the most part opposed to God's Word and faith. These are indeed a road which bypasses God, which is strongly forbidden in the First Commandment, which presses on the conscience with the hard threat of the law.

20. All such things would be too lengthy to explain here; therefore we let it rest. Hopefully, it is clearly enough brought to light in everyone's understanding so that they sufficiently comprehend what a danger is stored in our conscience. There was no other way for us to avoid this than by telling everything and, "Touch the unclean no more," as the Prophet Isaiah says in chapter 52, verse 12. . . .

29. Die andere Ursache, darum wir Klosterleben verlassen müssen, ist diese, dieweil wir, wie oben angezeigt, aus göttlicher Schrift nun erkennen, daß der Glaube das einige Werk unserer Seligkeit ist; desgleichen auch der Unglaube die einige Ursache unserer Verdammniß. So sind wir aus dem würdigen Wort GOttes auch deß berichtet, daß der Glaube im Herzen nicht genug ist zur Seligkeit, sondern es muß auch dabei sein ein öffentlich Bekenntniß, mit Verleugnen sein selbst. Denn also sagt Christus Matth. 10, 32. 33.: "Wer mich bekennen wird vor den Menschen, den will ich bekennen vor meinem Vater im Himmel. Wer mich vor den Menschen verleugnen wird, den will ich verleugnen vor meinem Vater im Himmel"; Luc. 9, 26.: "Wer sich aber mein und meiner Rede schämen wird, deß wird sich des Menschen Sohn auch schämen, wenn er kommen wird in seiner Herrlichkeit"; Paulus, Röm. 10, 10.: "So man mit dem Herzen glaubet, so wird man rechtfertig; so man aber mit dem Munde bekennet, so wird man selig."...

35. Derhalben, wie sollten wir entschuldigt sein, so wir die Mutter Christi und viel andere Heilige über ihn mit göttlicher Verehrung anbeten und ihnen göttliche Namen geben und auflegen; welches täglich geschieht in unsern Horis und Gebeten? Wir fürchten, wir werden der Schläge nicht können überhoben sein, so wir hierinne den Willen unsers HErrn wissen, und thun den nicht, Luc. 12, 47. Wiewohl uns niemand also vernehmen soll, daß wir die werthe Mutter Christi und die auserwählten Freunde GOttes dermaßen wollten gelästert, oder ihre Ehre wollten entzogen haben; sondern wir reden von der Ehre, die, GOtt allein zuständig, keiner Creatur soll gegeben werden. Von ihnen bekennen wir wohl, daß sie sind gewesen Tempel und Wohnung GOttes (1 Cor. 3, 16.) durch den Glauben, und eben sie sind es, die Werkzeuge, die GOtt zu seiner Herrlichkeit gebraucht hat, und seine großmächtigen Werke und Thaten in ihnen beweiset, auf daß wir durch solche Exempel gestärkt würden.

36. Auch gleichermaßen also, wie sie durch Glauben und Hoffnung selig werden, ebenso sinds, die uns haben vorgetragen die Exempel eines armen Geistes; derhalben sie sich aller Ding entblößen und allein GOtt die Ehre und Preis geben. Solch Exempel ist uns klar vorgebildet in der würdigen Mutter Christi, der Jungfrau Maria, wie Luc. 1, 42., da sie von Elisabeth ward ausgeschrieen eine Gesegnete über alle Weiber, sammt der gebenedeieten Frucht ihres Leibes, entblößt und äußert sie sich sein gänzlich, und wirft es auf GOtt. ... Welches

29. The second reason that we must leave convent life is this: As pointed out above, we now recognize from holy Scripture that faith is the only work [necessary for] our salvation; similarly, unbelief is the only reason for our damnation. So we are also informed by the esteemed Word of God that faith in the heart is not enough for salvation but there must also be a public confession, with a denial of self. For Christ also said (Matt. 10:32-33): "Who confesses me before men, that person will I confess before my Father in heaven. Whoever denies me before men, that one will I deny before my Father in heaven." Luke 9:26: "Whoever is ashamed of me and of my words, the Son of Man will be ashamed of when he comes to his glory." Paul in Romans 10:10: "When one believes with the heart, so is one justified; when one confesses with the mouth, so is one saved.". . .

35. For that reason, how shall we be pardoned if we worship the Mother of Christ and many other saints with divine reverence instead of him [i.e., Christ], and give and apply divine names to them, which happens daily [in the convent] in our hours and prayers? We fear we cannot be spared blows if we know our Lord's will in these matters and do not do it (Luke 12:47). Although nobody should speak ill of the worthy Mother of Christ and the chosen friends of God to any extent or take away their honor, we speak of the honor that is due to God alone and should be given to no creature. We, however, truly confess that they [i.e., Mary and the saints] are the temple and dwelling place of God (1 Cor. 3:16) through faith; and they are even the instruments that God has used to his glory and exhibited in them his mighty works and deeds so that we are strengthened through such examples.

36. At the same time, because they are saved through faith and hope, they have carried forth the example, divested themselves of everything and given honor and praise to God alone. Such an example is clearly modeled for us in the worthy Mother of Christ, the Virgin Mary (Luke 1:42). When Elizabeth proclaimed her as blessed over all women along with the blessed fruit of her womb, she separated herself from and placed herself outside of this completely, casting it all on God. ... Many

Exempel auch uns viel Heilige deß alten und neuen Testaments haben
vorgegeben, darinne billig GOtt in ihnen gelobt wird, der solches in
ihnen über und wider die Natur gewirkt hat, und uns zuständig,
solchem Exempel nachzufolgen...

39. Die dritte Ursache ist diese, Christus im Evangelio, Matth. 22,
37., da er anzeucht Mose im fünften Buch, am sechsten Capitel, in
diesem Spruch (V. 5.): "Du sollst lieben GOtt deinen HErrn von
ganzem Herzen, von ganzer Seele und von allen Kräften." In welchem
Gebot er nicht allein das äußerliche Werk fordert, sondern den ganzen
Menschen innerlich und äußerlich mit alle seinem Vermögen.
Dasselbige deutet er auch weiter Matth. 5, 20., da er sagt: "Es sei
denn eure Gerechtigkeit besser, denn der Schriftgelehrten und
Pharisäer, so möget ihr nicht in das Himmelreich kommen." In
welchem ganzen Capitel hernach sagt Christus, daß bei uns Christen
das äußerliche Werk ohne das Herz vor GOtt nicht gelten soll, sondern
es sei das Gesetz übertreten, so nicht da ist ein freiwilliger Geist, denn,
wie Röm. 7, 14., "das Gesetz ist geistlich" u.; demnach will es im
Geist verbracht werden...

42. Die vierte Ursach unsers Abschieds ist die: Wir haben Matthäi
4, 4., daß Christus sagt: "Der Mensch wird nicht allein vom Brod
leben, sondern von einem jeglichen Wort, das durch den Mund
GOttes gehet." Solches, dieweil es Christus, die göttliche Wahrheit,
selbst sagt, daß unser Leben hange an dem Wort GOttes, welches er
auch weiter erklärt Joh. 6, 51.: "Ich bin das lebendige Brod vom
Himmel kommen; wer von diesem Brod essen wird, der wird leben
in Ewigkeit", müssen wir es bekennen.

43. So denn nun unser ewig Leben an dem Wort GOttes hänget,
und allein, die ihm gehorchen, das Leben können erhalten, wie
Christus im Johanne an obengenannter Stelle anzeigt, so stimmen
wir mit ihm, daß wir unsern armen verschmachteten Seelen, so
hungrig und durstig sind, können keine Stärke noch Errettung finden,
denn allein bei dem würdigen Wort GOttes, so allein unser Heil und
Trost ist (Apost. 13, 26. Ps. 119, 92.). So kann ein jeder bedenken,
daß Schwachheit und Verschmachtung eines tödtlichen Leibes
allermeist daher komme, so er den Brauch der Speise nicht haben
kann. Und wer wollte sagen, daß ein Leib, der eine ganze Woche nur
einmal gespeist würde, bei seiner natürlichen Kraft könnte erhalten
werden, vornehmlich so er mit schweren Lasten und großer Arbeit
beladen wäre?

saints of the Old and New Testaments have presented examples of this type to us, in which God is approvingly praised in them, because he accomplished things in them which were greater than and opposed to their natures. It is appropriate for us to follow such examples. . . .

39. The third reason [for leaving the convent] is this: Christ in the Gospel of Matthew (22:37) cites Moses' fifth book, sixth chapter (v. 5) in this saying: "You should love God your Lord with your whole heart, with your whole soul, and with all your strength." In this command, he not only refers to external work but to the whole person, inwardly and outwardly, with all his abilities. He also means this in Matthew 5:20 where he says: "Unless your righteousness is better than the scribes and pharisees, you may not come into the kingdom of Heaven." In the whole chapter which follows, Christ says that for us Christians, external works without the heart will not matter before God, but it is violating the law when there is no free-willing spirit, as in Romans 7:14: "The law is spiritual," etc., therefore it will be accomplished in the Spirit. . . .

42. The fourth reason for our departure is this: We have Matthew 4:4, where Christ says: "A person will not live by bread alone but from every word that goes forth from God's mouth." Thus Christ, who is divine truth, himself says that our life depends on the Word of God, which he explains further in John 6:51: "I have come as the living bread from heaven; who eats of this bread will live eternally," so we must confess it.

43. So because our eternal life now depends on the Word of God and only those who obey him can obtain [eternal] life, (as Christ pointed out in John, in the aforementioned place) we agree with him that we cannot find strength nor deliverance for our poor languishing souls, so hungry and thirsty, except from the precious Word of God that alone is our salvation and consolation. (Acts 13:26; Ps. 119:92). Everyone understands that weakness and hunger come to a mortal body if it cannot have food regularly. And who would say that a body that is fed only once in a whole week could be saved by its own natural power, especially if it were laden with difficult burdens and heavy work?

44. Was ist denn zu sagen von einer edlen Seele, welche von Art ihrer Natur ganz leichtlich versehrt wird, geschwächt und getödtet, so sie ihrer Speise, so ihre Kraft und Leben ist, muß beraubt sein, nämlich, des Worts GOttes, ohne welches sie nicht leben kann, zuvor, so sie also belästigt wird mit so viel ungewissen Dingen, welche ihr Gift und der Tod sind?...

46. Die fünfte Ursache, so uns belästigt in unserm Gewissen, ist diese. Wir haben oben angezeigt im dritten Artikel, daß alle unsere Werke so bezwungen und ohn GOttes Befehl herfließen aus einem unlustigen Herzen, und derhalben nachfolglich ein bös Gewissen gespürt wird, welches wir aufs höchste uns beschwert sinden in Empfahung des heiligen Sacraments des Leibes Christi, zu welchen wir oftmals im Jahr, als nämlich, zu vier und zwanzig Malen, ausgenommen die eigenerwählten Tage, gezwungen sind mit Gebot, einer sei gleich geschickt, wie er wolle, so hilft auch keine Entschuldigung dafür, es liege auf dem Gewissen, was da wolle, so muß es strack gehen.

47. So aber ein solch Sacrament fordert eine hungrige Seele, so ihre Noth erkennt, derhalben sie allda Trost und Hülfe zu suchen selbwillig und begierig hinzugehen soll, wie denn die Worte seiner Einsetzung lauten, und Paulus 1 Cor. 11, 27. sagt: "Wer da unwürdig von diesem Brod isset, oder vom Kelche des HErrn trinket, der wird schuldig an dem Leibe und Blut des HErrn." Und hernach an derselben Statt setzt er große erschreckliche Dräuung über solche, so dies heilige Sacrament unwürdiglich empfahen...

49. Die sechste Ursache: Joh. 13, 34. sagt Christus: "Ein neu Gebot gebe ich euch, daß ihr euch unter einander liebet, gleichwie ich euch geliebet habe"; und Matth. 22, 37. 40.: "Du sollst lieben GOtt deinen HErrn von ganzem Herzen, von ganzer Seele, von ganzem Gemüthe. Dies is das vornehmste und größeste Gebot. Das andere aber ist dem gleich: Du sollst deinen Nächsten lieben als dich selbst. In diesen zweien Geboten hanget das ganze Gesetz und die Propheten." Und Paulus zun Römern 12, 18.: "Ist's möglich, so viel an euch ist, so haltet mit jedermann Friede."

50. Solche Liebe und Friede können wir dieser Stelle und Ortes nicht spüren, sondern eben das Widerspiel, und daß diese Worte Christi in vollem Schwang gehen, Matth. 10, 36.: "Des Menschen Feinde werden seine eigenen Hausgenossen sein." Und Luc. 12, 52. 53.: "Ihr werden fünfe in einem Hause spännig sein, drei wider zwei,

44. What is then to be said about a precious soul, which because of its nature can be easily led astray, weakened, and killed? What if it is robbed of its food, its strength and life, that is, the Word of God, without which it cannot live, especially if it is burdened with so many uncertain things which are poisonous and deadly for it?. . .

46. The fifth reason that troubles us in our conscience is this: We have demonstrated above in the third paragraph that all our works which are forced and without God's command originate in a reluctant heart, and, because of this we later experience a bad conscience. We find this burdens us to the highest degree in the reception of the holy sacrament of Christ's body, to which we are often forced to go many times during the year — that is, twenty-four times — along with those days we choose to go. [One goes] whether one is fit to go or not, and no excuses help; this lies heavily on one's conscience.

47. But such a sacrament demands a hungry soul, who confesses her need, and for that reason goes there freely in order to seek consolation and help. As the words of institution for the sacrament state, and as Paul (1 Cor. 11:27) says: "Whoever eats unworthily of this bread or drinks the cup of the Lord, that one will be guilty of the body and blood of the Lord." And afterwards in the same chapter he sets out terrible torments for those who partake of this holy sacrament unworthily...

49. The sixth reason: [In] John 13:34 Christ says: "I give you a new commandment, that you love one another as I have loved you," and in Matthew 22:37-40: "You should love God your Lord with the whole heart, with the whole soul, with the whole mind. This is the foremost and greatest commandment. But the other is similar: You should love your neighbor as yourself. The whole law and prophets hinge on these two commandments." And Paul in Romans 12:18: "If possible, as much as is in you, be at peace with everyone."

50. Such love and peace we cannot feel in this place and situation [i.e., the convent] but rather the opposite, for the following Word of Christ operates there in full swing — Matthew 10:36: "One's enemies will be from his own household." And Luke 12:52-53: "In one house there will be five divided, three against two and two against

und zwei wider drei. Es wird sich der Vater setzen wider den Sohn,
und der Sohn wider den Vater, und die Mutter wider die Tochter,
und die Tochter wider die Mutter"; and so solches geschehen soll in
einem kleinen Hause, da nur ihr fünf bei einander sind, kann ein
jeder bedenken, was denn in einer groflen Versammlung geschehen
sollte, da ihr bei sieben und siebenzig Personen versammelt sind.
Derhalben wir uns schlechts müssen davon wenden: nicht darum,
daß wir Verfolgung nicht leiden wollten, welcher wir uns an keinem
Orte nicht äußern können noch wollen, sondern weil unsere Gewissen
hierinnen nicht können befriedet werden. . .

55. Die siebente Ursache, so uns bewegt, Klosterleben zu verlassen,
ist diese. Wir haben allenthalben in göttlicher Schrift, daß unser Leben
allenthalben soll dahin gerichtet sein, daß einer dem andern die Hand
reiche und ihm diene, welches zu bestätigen, sich Christus selbst zu
einem Exempel vorstellet, Joh. 13, 15.: "Ein Exempel habe ich euch
gegeben, daß ihr zugleich thut, wie ich euch gethan habe", welches
er auch gethan, Marc. 10, 45., und Röm. 12, 5.: "Wir viele sind Ein
Leib, aber unter einander ist einer des andern Glied" u. 1 Cor. 14, V.
26.: "Laßt's alles geschehen zur Besserung."

56. Demnach, so wir in eine solche Stelle gesetzt sind, darinne wir
niemand können dienen, sondern ihrer vielen ärgerlich sind, ist uns
nicht zu rathen, ein solches zu vermeiden? Denn es ja öffentlich am
Tage ist, wie oben angezeigt, daß wir nicht überein gesinnt sind.
Denn sie achten auf menschliche Gesetze und stellen ihre Seligkeit
drein; wir aber können in keinen Wege darinne vertröstet und
befriedet sein, derhalben können wir auch in äußerlichen Werken
nicht übereinstimmen allenthalben.

57. Solches aber weiter anzuzeigen, können wir nicht thun, denn
durch Exempel, als nämlich, so sie gewohnt sind, lange Gebet
vorzuwenden, in welchen sie etliche Aberglauben und Uebung haben,
in welchen wir erkennen GOtt Unehre zu geschehen, sammt seinem
würdigen Wort, und derhalben von uns nachgelassen, ist ihnen
ärgerlich. Solche und dergleichen Fälle wären sehr viel, welche zu
lang zu erzählen würden, welches auch von unnöthen, wiewohl wir
uns ihnen gerne in allen Dingen, so nicht groß wider GOtt sind,
hätten wollen vergleichen, und unseres schwachen Vermögens auch
gethan haben, so viel unsere Schwachheit hat können tragen und
dulden den Schwachen zu Dienste, haben wir doch können spüren,
daß wir uns um die andern wenig oder nichts verdient haben, und ist

three. It will place father against son and son against father, mother against daughter and daughter against mother"; and if this shall happen in a little house where only five are found with one another, everyone can think what shall happen in a great assembly where seven and seventy persons are gathered. For that reason we must simply turn away from this: not because we did not want to suffer persecution — which we could not nor would not speak about anywhere — but because our conscience could not be at peace here. . . .

55. The seventh reason that stirred us to abandon convent life is this: Everywhere in sacred Scripture it is written that our life should be directed toward reaching out our hands to one another and serving them. To confirm this, Christ presents himself as an example (John 13:15): "I have given you an example so that you do the same as I have done for you," which he also did in Mark 10:45 and Romans 12:5: "We many are one body and individually members of one another," etc. 1 Corinthians 14:26: "Let everything happen for improvement."

56. Therefore, if we are put in such a place where we cannot serve anybody but are very vexed, is it not advisable to leave such a place? Yes, it is clear, as noted above, that we were not in agreement. For they pay attention to human laws and place their salvation therein; in no way could we be consoled and made peaceful through these means, so that for that reason we could also never agree about external works.

57. We cannot talk about this further, but we can show examples, such as: They are accustomed to prescribe long prayers, in which they have some superstitions and practices which we acknowledge dishonor God and his esteemed Word. We thus leave them out, which annoys them. These and similar cases were very numerous, too long and unnecessary to explain. We had wanted to reconcile ourselves to those things which were not too much against God, and had done this as much as our weak capabilities would allow, as much as our weakness could bear and stand in order to serve the weak. But we could still tell that we have done little or nothing for others. But "doing" was a

Thun eben so viel gewesen als Lassen; haben dennoch mit
Beschwerung der Gewissen uns allein müssen leben, so wir doch
durch das Gewissen überzeugt sind Schuldiger aller, nämlich, durch
die Liebe, welche uns unterweist, einem jeden zu dienen, zu helfen
und rathen, welches wir auch oft nöthig erkannt haben und gerne
gethan hätten, so es uns verhangen und nachgelassen wäre worden.
58. Hätten auch oft gewußt, kranken Leuten Rettung zu thun mit
Heimsuchung, Wartung und Handreichnung; desgleichen auch
sterbenden Leuten mit Gesellschaft zu leisten, sie zu trösten und
stärkem mit dem Wort GOttes, welches zu der Zeit aufs höchste
vonnöthen ist; und hätten ihrer auch wohl gewußt, die allein ohn
allen menschlichen Trost von dieser Welt geschieden sind; ist uns
aber nicht verhangen. So wissen wir auch Leute, so unsers Raths zu
brauchen, wiewohl geringe, auch höchlich begehrt hätten, so sie mit
uns hätten können reden unverhinderlich anderer Leute. Es hat nicht
können geschehen, solche Dienste zu erzeigen bei denen, so bei uns
wohnende sind gewesen, hat auch nicht können geschehen, förderlich
zu trösten die betrübten und schwachen Gewissen, so ganz trostlos
gewesen sind und göttliches Trostes unerfahren und unwissend,
welche mit Verfolgung, Dräuen und Schmach, so sie haben müssen
leiden, sind abgeschreckt und gescheuet worden, daß sie uns auch
nicht wohl haben dürfen ansehen, auch vor uns geflohen sind, wo
sie uns nur gesehen haben.

59. Aus welchem allen, lieben Freunde, habt ihr zu ermessen, mit
welchem guten Gewissen wir dabei sein könnten. Wer könnte uns
nun versichern, daß wir, in solchem Falle entschuldigt, könnten
GOttes Urtheil entfliehen? Matth. 25, 41. 45., da Christus solche
verurtheilt zu dem ewigen Feuer, und sagt: "Wahrlich, ich sage euch,
was ihr nicht gethan habt einem unter diesen Geringsten, das habt
ihr auch wir nicht gethan." Hieneben, so wir ihnen in dem hätten
können dienen, nämlich, in den täglichen Aufsätzen und Ceremonien,
welches wir doch vor GOttes Augen, der alle Dinge siehet,
Schwachheit halben unsers Leibs gar nicht vermocht haben, wie
unsere Gewissen bezeugen werden auf des HErrn Tag, wollten wir
auch über die Kräfte und Vermögen gethan haben. . . .

66. Daß wir aber hierinne so viel überflüssiger Worte braucht haben,
ist aus der Ursache geschehen, daß wir oftmals verstanden haben,
daß etliche sich daran geärgert haben, und ist ihnen so schimpflich
und lächerlich gewesen, so etliche, die vor uns aus den Klöstern gezogen

matter of "being permitted to," and now we must live alone with a burdened conscience. We are convinced through our conscience that we are all debtors, that is, through the love that instructs us to serve each other, to help and advise. We often necessarily recognized this and would have willingly done so, if it [the rules] had been relaxed and we had been allowed to.

58. We would also have been able to do pleasant things for ill people, such as visitations, care, and charity, and to provide dying people with companions, to console them and strengthen them with the word of God, which at that point [in their lives] is the thing they need the most; and we would have been able to [console] those who are leaving this world without any human care; but this was not permitted to us. We also know people who needed our advice, sometimes in small things, and who grievously requested that they be allowed to speak with us without being bothered by other people. We were not allowed to do such services to those who lived with us. We were also not allowed to comfort the afflicted and weak souls, who were completely without hope and inexperienced and unknowledgeable about God's consolation. They were scared away and afraid because of the persecution, threats and disgrace that they would have suffered [if they had spoken to us], and so didn't want to be seen by us, running away from us whenever they saw us.

59. From all of this, dear friends, you have to measure with what sort of a good conscience we could have remained there. Who could have assured us that we could have escaped God's judgment and been excused in this case? In Matthew 25:41, 45 Christ judges such ones to eternal fire and says: "Truly, I say to you, what you have not done for the least of these, you have not done for me. Besides, if we had been able to serve them, that is, in the daily traditions and ceremonies that before God's eyes (who sees all things) we were not capable of doing because of the weakness of our bodies (as our conscience will declare on the Lord's Day), we would also have done so with strength and capability. . . .

66. That we have used so many superfluous words herein occurs because we have ofttimes understood that some people have become angry at those who were drawn out of the convent before us, insult-

sind, alle diese Dinge in eine Summa weniger Worte gefaßt haben,
so sie gesagt haben: Sie vertrauen in Klöstern nicht selig zu werden.
Ja, wohl haben sie deß zu lachen, weil sie nicht wissen, was ein solch
Wort auf sich hat. Es sind wohl wenig Worte, haben aber ein weit
Bedenken.

67. Wir wären auch wohl also gesinnet, so uns einer sagen wollte,
er wäre in einen tiefen Sumpf gefallen, da das Wasser sammt dem
Unflath über ihm zusammengeschlagen wäre, und wo er sich nicht
daraus gearbeitet hätte, wäre er darinne ersoffen und erstickt: wir
wollten eines solchen auch wohl lachen, so wir nie befunden hätten,
wie tief und fährlich der Sumpf wäre, darein er gefallen wäre, ja wollten
noch wohl dazu sagen: Du sagst nicht wahr, weil du von Tiefe, von
Wasser und Schlamm sagst, und wir sehen der keines, denn nur ebene
Erde und einen lustigen grünen Boden; wie sollte unter dem solche
Fährlichkeit sein? Das macht alles das, daß wir die ängstliche Noth
des Todes nicht geschmeckt hätten, in welcher der gewesen wäre. Ja,
wohl könnten wir sein lachen; ihm aber, dem es widerfahren wäre,
hätten wir Sorge, würde es Ernst genug sein.

68. Eben dermaßen, lieben Freunde, gedenkt, daß uns überflüssiger
Ernst daran gelegen ist, so keinen Schimpf duldet, und denkt nur
nicht, daß ein solches geängstet Gewissen immermehr kann zu Friede
und Ruhe kommen, weder hie noch dort, es sei denn, daß es eine
solche schwere Last ablege; und seid ihr GOtt dankbar seiner Gnade,
daß er euch davor behütet hat, und habt auch Mitleidung mit denen,
so also schwerlich gefangen und belästigt sind, und richtet niemand
in diesem Fall; denn wer weiß, was einem jeglichen Herzen gebricht?
Denn eben hieher bequemt sich dies Sprüchwort: Es ist nicht alles
Gold, das gleißt. Denn wer wollte doch unter einem solchen
säuberlichen Schein menschlicher Heiligkeit eine solche große
Fährlichkeit suchen? Wir glaubten's auch nicht, wenn wir selber nicht
so tief darinne gesteckt hätten.

69. Hiemit wollen wir euch allesammt gebeten haben, lieben Brüder
und Schwestern in Christo, vor wen diese unsere Schrift kommen
wird, so wir mit eigener Hand, ohne aller Menschen Rath und Hülfe
geschrieben haben, da wir noch unter der babylonischen Gefängniß
gefangen und bestrickt waren, wolltet solcher unser wahrhaftigen
Bekenntniß Glauben geben und den allerhöchsten GOtt mit uns
preisen, der uns aus solcher Fährlichkeit erlöst hat; und durch die
Liebe des Geistes helft uns kämpfen mit Gebeten für uns, daß wir

ing and laughing at those who have said all of these things with only a few words. All they said was: They have no confidence of becoming holy in convents. Yes, others may have laughed at this because they do not know what such words mean. They may be just a few words, but they have a wide meaning.

67. We were also reminded that if someone says to us he has fallen into a deep swamp, where the water and filth together are defeating him and where he could not work himself out, where he is mired and stuck, we would also laugh at him if we never found out how deep and dangerous the swamp is into which he has fallen. Yes, we would probably say: You aren't speaking truly because you speak about the deep, about water and mud, but we see nothing except level ground and pleasant green earth; how could there be danger under these? This is so because we have not tasted the anguished need of death in which he has been. Yes, we would indeed laugh; but we should have worries about him to whom this has happened, for it would be very serious.

68. You may think, dear friends, that we are being too serious and are not able to suffer insults. But do not think that such an anguished conscience can come to peace and rest either here or there unless it sets down its heavy burden. Thank God for his grace, that he has watched over you and has sympathy for those who are caught and heavily burdened and judges no one in this case. For who knows what crushes each heart? Even here, the saying comforts: All that glitters is not gold. Who would look for such a great danger under such a neat appearance of human holiness? We would not have believed it ourselves had we not been so deeply stuck in it.

69. Herewith we will pray together for you, dear brothers and sisters in Christ, for whom this writing has been done. We have written with our own hand, without anyone's advice or help, that we were trapped and stuck under the Babylonian Captivity.[2] We wanted to give our truthful testimony of faith and praise the all-highest God who has delivered us from such danger; and through the love of the Spirit helps us battle with prayers for us, that all of us together may be

durch Christem allesammt mögen selig werden, Amen. Vollendet und
geschrieben mit unserer eigenen Hand, am 28. April 1528.

blessed in Christ. Amen. Completed and written with our own hand on April 28, 1528.

Notes

1. Because Ursula is a noblewoman, she speaks of herself in the plural throughout this text, in the same way that other rulers did.
2. Ursula is here using Luther's expression for the Catholic Church, as in his 1520 treatise *The Babyonian Captivity of the Christian Church.* She may have read this while still in the convent; there is good evidence that Lutheran works were smuggled in by the early 1520s.

Anna Sophia von Quedlinburg

Der treue Seelenfreund Christus Jesus mit nachdenklichen Sinn-gemahlden

Anna Sophia of Quedlinburg

The true soulfriend Jesus Christ with emblems to contemplate

Anna Sophia von Quedlinburg

Der Durchleuchtigen und Hochgebohrnen Fürstin unserer Gnädigen
hochgeehrtesten Frau Mutter Frauen Sophien Eleonoren Gebohrnen
aus dem ChurFürstlichen Hause zu Sachsen, Landgräfin zu Hessen,
Gräfin zu Catzenelnbogen, Dietz, Ziegenhain, Nidda, Isenburg und
Büdingen, etc.

Was wir an kindlich-demütigem Gehorsam und sonsten Liebes und
Gutes vermögen iederzeit bevor
Durchleuchtige, Hochgebohrne Chur-Fürstin, Gnädige Hoch-
geehrteste Groß-Frau-Mutter,
Durchleuchtiger, Hochgebohrner Fürst, Gnädiger Hochgeehrtester
Herr Vater,
Durchleuchtige, Hochgebohrne Fürstin, Gnädige Hochgeehrteste
Frau Mutter,
E. E. E. G. G. G. werden vielleicht wegen obhandener Schrift sich
etlicher massen zu verwundern veranlasset werden, insonderheit weil
wir, als ein schwacher Werkzeug, wie S. Petrus das weibliche Geschlecht
nennet, 1.Petr.3.v.7 uns so einer hohen Sachen unterfangen, und
unsere wenige, iedennoch Geistliche Gedanken dem überklugen
Urtheil dieser Welt öffentlich zu unterwerffen nicht scheu tragen,
wie denn auch eben dieses letztere uns fast abgeschrekket hätte unser
wohlgemeinetes Fürnehmen fortzusetzen. Aber weil wir, Gott Lob,
wissen, daß auch die allerheiligsten Leute vor denen übersichtigen
Klüglingen nicht gäntzlich haben können befrehet seyn, weswegen
wolten wir uns denn scheuen, so dieselbigen auch in unsern Sachen
etwas zu tadeln sucheten, die wir ohne dieß unserer Schwachheit uns
wohl bewust sind. Als die Gottselige Hanna am allerandächtigsten zu
GOTT in ihrem Hertzen seuftzete, da meinete der Priester Eli sie
währe trunken, und sprach zu ihr: Wie lange wiltu trunken seyn. Laß
den Wein von dir kommen, den du bey dir hast. 1.Sam. 1 vers.13.14.
Ist dieses der Gottseeligen Hanna widerfahren, und zwar von einem
Priester, wie solten wir uns denn von dieser Welt etwas bessers
einzubilden haben? Damit aber E. E. E. Gn. Gn. Gn. die Ursachen,
welche uns zu Verfertigung dieses Büchleins angereitzet, nicht
verhalten werden möchten, als ist deroselben erste und fürnehmste
GOTTES Befehl, Kraft welches ER alle Menschen, so wohl Weibes-
als Mannespersonen, zu seiner Liebe und zu seinem Lobe verbunden.

Anna Sophia of Quedlinburg

The enlightened and highborn princess, our gracious, highly honored Mother Sophia Eleonora, Born from the Electoral House of Saxony, Landgravess of Hesse, Countess of Catzenelnbogen, Dietz, Ziegenhain, Nidda, Isenburg, and Büdingen, etc.

What we attempt in childlike, humble obedience and the usual love and kindness as at any former time:
Enlightened, highborn Electoress, gracious, highly honored Grandmother;
Enlightened, highborn Prince, gracious, highly honored Father;
Enlightened, highborn Princess, gracious, highly honored Mother:
Perhaps E. E. E. G. G. G.[1] will cause us to be chastised because of some measure of overly forceful writing, especially since we, although a poor instrument as St. Peter called the weaker sex (1 Peter 3:7), dare such high matters. And our few spiritual thoughts often do not bear up to a timid submission to the conceited judgment of this world, for this latter had almost nearly deterred us from continuing our community's primary undertaking. But because we (Praise God!) know that even the holiest of people cannot wholly be freed from those who are superficially clever, we wanted to hesitate, for they would also seek to censure something in our activities, which we certainly are aware of without this our weakness. When the divinely blessed Hanna sighed with great esteem to God in her heart, it appeared to the priest Eli that she was drunk. And he said to her: "How long will you be drunk? Put the wine that has beset you away from yourself" (1 Sam. 1:13-14). If this happened to the blessed Hanna, and indeed from a priest, how then should we have imagined something better for us from this world? Therewith, E. E. E. Gn. Gn. Gn., the cause that impels us to the construction of this little book may not be suppressed, but is itself first and foremost God's command. His authority obliges all people, women as well as men, to his love and his praise.

Dannenhero saget auch David in seinem 148. Ps. v. 11,12,13. Ihr Könige auf Erden und alle Leute, Fürsten und alle Richter auf Erden, Jünglinge und Jungfrauen, Alten mit den Jungen, sollen loben den Nahmen des Herren, denn sein Nahm allein ist hoch, sein Lob gehet so weit, Himmel und Erden ist. Jungfrauen, saget David, sollen (es stehet nicht in ihrem Belieben, sonder es ist ihnen von dem Allerhöchsten anbefohlen) eben so wohl den Nahmen des HERREN loben, als andere Leute. Und darzu haben sie auch genugsame Ursache; Sintemal sie eben so wohl von Gott dem Vater erschaffen, von Gott dem Sohne mit seinem theuren Rosinfarben Blute erlöset, und von Gott dem heiligen Geiste zu Miterben der Gnade geheiliget worden. Die Weibesbilder tragen eben so wohl das Haupt empor, zu bedeuten, daß sie nicht weniger als andere Menschen den Himmelanschauen, und des Himmels Schöpfer ehren sollen, daß sie nicht weniger als andere Menschen zu hohen und himmlischen Betrachtangen gebohren seyen, ihrer natürlichen Schwachheit zu steuren, und den müßigen Sinn zu beschäftigen, saget die berühmte Niederländerin Anna Maria Schurmannin in ihrer Erklärung von des Weiblichen Geschlechtes Fähigkeit zum Studieren. Zu solchem Lobe vermahnet auch der heilige Augustinus das Frauenzimmer wenn er saget: Laudate (O virgines) dulcius, quem cogitatis uberius. O ihr Jungfrauen, lobet den (er redet aber von niemand anders als von unserm getreuesten Seelenfreunde Christo Jesu, wie aus folgenden zu ersehen) mit lieblicher Stimme, and den ihr so fleißig gedenket, sperate felicius, cui servitis instantius, lebet auf den in desto vergnügter Hofnung, dem ihr so beständig dienet; amate ardentius, cui placetis attentius, liebet den desto inbrünstiger, dem ihr so wolgefallet. Vos afferetis ad nuptias agni canticum novum, Ihr werdet die Hochzeit des Lammes mit einem neuen Liede verehren, Insuper sequemini agnum, quod nemo eum sequi vel audeat, vel valeat, Ja, ihr werdet dem Lamme biß dahin folgen, dahin niemand, ohne die in wahren Glauben Ihn beständig geliebet haben, kommen darf oder kan. Quod putamus eum ire? in saltus & prata, ubi credo sunt grandia gaudia, non gaudia seculi hujus vana. Wo meinen wir aber wohl, da das Lam solle hingehen. Auf die allerlustigsten Wiesen, da, wie ich gewißlich glaube, die höchsten Freuden seyn werden, da nicht solche vergängliche Freuden seyn werden, wie in dieser Welt. Gaudia virginum Christi de Christo, in Christo, cum Christo, per Christum, propter Christum. Die Jungfrauen Christi werden sich freuen über Christo, in Christo, mit

In that regard, David said in his 148th Psalm, verses 11, 12, 13: "Your kings of the earth and all people, princes and all judges of the earth, young men and young women, old men along with youths, should praise the name of the Lord because his name alone is exalted, his praise issues from the breadth and width of heaven and earth." Young women, said David, should fully praise the name of the Lord even as other people should. (This does not stem from their own gratification but is commanded of them.) They have sufficient cause for that praise since they are created as well by God the Father, redeemed by God the Son through his priceless rose-colored blood, and sanctified by the Holy Spirit through grace. Women carry their heads on high [i.e., at the top of their bodies] just as much [as men], which means that they should look to heaven and honor the creator of the heavens no less than other people, that they are therefore no less born to high and heavenly considerations than other people are. They must put a check on their natural weakness and occupy their idle minds, says the well-known Netherlander, Anna Maria von Schurman,[2] in her explanation of the female sex's capacity for studies. St. Augustine also exhorted women to such praise when he said: "Praise, (O virgins,) more sweetly, [him] to whom your thoughts are more fully devoted."[3] O you young women, praise (he spoke about none other than our truest soulfriend, Christ Jesus, as can be gathered from the following) with loving voices (him) whom you so diligently contemplate. "Hope in him more eagerly, whom you serve more eagerly." Come to life in the more joyful hope [of him] whom you so constantly serve. "Love more ardently [him] whom you more attentively please." Love more ardently [him] whom you so fully please. "You shall offer a new song at the marriage of the Lamb." You honor the marriage of the Lamb with a new song. "From above proceeds the Lamb where no one but you either dares or is able to follow." Yes, you will follow the Lamb to that place where no one without true faith in him is steadfastly loved and allowed to or able to come. "Where do we think he goes, to what heights and meadows? Where I believe the greatest delights are not the empty joys of the world that are vain folly." Where do we mean that the Lamb shall come forth? In the glad meadows where, as I certainly believe, the highest joys will not be those transitory joys of this world. "The delight of the virgins of Christ, from Christ, in Christ, with Christ, through Christ, and because of Christ." Virgins of Christ will rejoice over Christ, in Christ, with Christ, through Christ, and

Christo, durch Christum, und wegen Christi. Wie solten wir denn
nun unsern treuen SeelenFreund Christum Jesum üm solcher Freuden
willen nicht loben? Zweytens hat uns zu diesem Werk angereitzet das
Christliche Exempel so viel heiligen und lobwürdigsten Frauen-
zimmers. Man pfleget ins gemein darfür zu halten, daß einem
Menschen nichts mehr zu Gemühte gehe, oder zu etwas bewegen
könne, als die Exempel, und dieses verhält sich auch also in der That
und Wahrheit. Wann wir derowegen ansehen die Mutter aller
Lebendigen die Evam so ist sie nechst GOTT in der heiligen Schrift
die erste, die dem verheissenen Schlangentreter zu Ehren ihren Mund
aufthäte und ausruffete: Ich habe den Mann, den Herren. Und
wiewohl sie in der Person damaln irrete, so war doch ihr Wille gut,
Gen. 4.v.1. Hat nicht Debora ihren GOTT mit einem solchen
herrlichen Lobgesang verehret, welcher zu befinden Jud.5. Wie frölich
war doch die Hanna in ihrem Hertzen, da sie Gott dem Herrn zu
Ehren frolokkete? 1 Sam. 2. Setzete nicht die Judith GOTT zu Ehren
ein neues Lied auf, als sie die Stadt Bethulia von der Assyrer Heerlager
befrehet hatte? Judith, 16. Wen beweget nicht zu gleicher
Hertzensfreude das auserlesene Magnificat der H. Jungfrau-Mutter
Gottes Maria? Luc. 1.v.47. Wie solten denn diese Exempel nicht
auch uns zu ihrer Nachfolge anmahnen, zumalen weil Christus
erinnert, daß wir uns zu denen klugen Jungfrauen halten sollen, auf
daß, wenn ER als unser himlischer Seelen-Bräutigam kommen wird, wir
möchten bereit seyn ihm zu dienen, und nicht sampt denen Thörichten
aus dem Hochzeithause ausgeschlossen werden/ Matt. 25/10.

Daß wir aber eben von der geistlichen Seelenfreundschaft zu
handeln uns fürgenommen, ist deswegen geschehen. Es hat GOtt
der heilige Geist, durch dessen Trieb die heiligen Männer GOttes
geredet und geschrieben haben, in keinem Buche der Göttlichen
Schrift dem Frauenzimmer so vielfältige Ehre erwiesen, als in dem
Hohenlied Salomonis, allda ER durch und durch die Christliche
Kirche, wie auch eine iede gläubige Seele einer Braut vergleichet. In
Betrachtung dessen haben wir GOTT dem heiligen Geiste und der
gantzen hochgebenedeyeten Drey-Einigkeit wiederum zu Ehren eine
Materiam, aus dem besagten Hohenliede Salomonis auserlesen, und
weil insonderheit in demselben fast nichts so oft widerhohlet wird
als: Mein Freund: Meine Freundin; Als haben wir Gott dem
Allerhöchsten zu Lobe, der uns arme elende Menschen so hoch
gewürdiget, und zu seinen Freunden angenommen, vor allen andern

because of Christ. Why should we therefore not want to praise our true soul's friend, Christ Jesus, with such joy? Second, the Christian example of so many holy and most praise-worthy women has led us to this work. One generally is accustomed to think, that nothing better reminds a person, or can move him or her to do something, than an example. This is held both in deed and in truth. Because of this, when we consider the mother of all the living, Eve, she is the first next to God in holy Scripture who reacted and called out from her mouth to honor the promised serpent-treader [i.e., Adam]: "I have the man of the Lord." And, although she erred personally at the time, even so her inclination was good (Gen.4:1). Did Debora not venerate her God with the most glorious song of praise to be found (Jud. 5)? How joyful, too, was Hanna's heart that she rejoiced to honor God the Lord (1 Sam. 2). Did not Judith offer a new song to honor God when she freed the city of Bethulia from the Assyrian army encampment (Jth. 16)? Who is not moved to the same joyful heart of the exquisite Magnificat of the holy Virgin Mother of God, Mary (Luke 1:47)? How could this example not remind us to follow after her, especially since Christ enjoined us to hold fast to [the example of] the wise virgins, to be prepared when he as our heavenly soul's bridegroom will come. We must be prepared to serve him and not be locked out from the wedding house together with the foolish (Matt. 25:10).

That is the reason which impels us to engage in the soul's spiritual friendship. God the Holy Spirit, through whose urging the holy men of God have spoken and written, rendered women multiple honors in no book of divine Scripture as much as in his Book of divine Scripture, rendered women multiple honors, as in the exalted Song of Solomon in which he throughout compares the Christian church and each believing soul to a bride. In view of that, we have the occasion again to honor God the Holy Spirit and the entire highly giving Trinity, choosing a piece from the aforementioned Song of Solomon, because especially in this almost nothing is so often repeated as, "My male friend, my female friend." Then we have God the All-highest to praise, who so greatly dignified us poor miserable people and accepted us before all others as his friends, and let us engage in the soul's spiritual friend-

vonder Geistlichen Seelen-Freundschaft zu handeln uns belieben
lassen; und zwar auf folgende Weise: Erstlich wird der feste Schluß
gemachet, daß niemand, er sey wer er wolle, ohn allein CHristus
JEsus ein rechter treuer Freund sey, zu dem man in seinen
Tausendängsten und Seelennöhten sicherlich fliehen könne. Zu noch
mehrer Bekräftigung dessen, werden alsobald darauf denen andern
Freunden, als dem Teuffel, der Welt, und dem menschlichen Fleisch
und Blute, ihre betrügliche Larven abgezogen, mit denen sie die
Menschen unter dem Nahmen der Freundschaft zu verführen
gedenken. Damit aber die Hoheit dieser geistlischen Seelenfreundschaft in etwas erhellen möge, als haben wir in der fünften Betrachtung
dargethan, wer denn dieser unser Seelenfreund sey, nehmlichen
CHristus JEsus, der wahre wesentliche Gott von Ewigkeit zu Ewigkeit;
In der sechsten Betrachtung aber haben wir erwiesen wer wir im
Gegentheil seyn, nehmlich arme, elende, sterbliche Menschen, die
wir mit unsern Sünden GOttes Zorn und Ungnade, zeitlichen Tod
und ewiges Verdamniß verdienet haben. Damit man aber auch wissen
möge, wie man denn zu solcher geistlichen Seelenfreundschaft
gelangen konne, als haben wir in denen folgenden Betrachtungen
die Mittel darzu gezeiget, als nehmlich die andächtige Anhörung des
Göttlichen Worts, den Gebrauch der hochheiligen Sacramenten, und
den wahren seeligmachenden Glauben. Endlich folget darauf der
herrliche Nutz, welchen diese geistliche Seelenfreundschaft mit sich
bringet. Die Lehrgedichte, welche mit untergemischet worden, sind
zum Theil aus der heiligen Schrift, zum Theil aus denen Patribus
und anderen genommen, zum Theil von uns selber gedichtet worden.
Doch ist dieses bey denenselben zu erinnern, daß man sie, wie auch
die Emblemata, nicht weiter deuten solle, als die gesetzten Schranken
zulassen, sonst würden oft ungereimte Sachen daraus erfolgen. Die
Patres, und andere Autores, die wir hierinnen oftermals angeführet
belangende, so bekennen wir zwar freywillig, daß wir selbige nicht
allesampt selbsten durchlesen, dennoch haben wir solche Gelegenheit
an der Hand gehabt, daß uns die fürnehmsten Sachen aus denenselben
etlicher Massen sind bekant worden. Und eben dieses Büchlein haben
nun E. E. E. Gn. Gn. Gn. wir hiermit demühtig-gehorsamst
untergeben wollen, in Betrachtung, daß wir nechst GOtt niemand
auf Erden mehr zu danken und zu geben schuldig sind, als E. E. E.
Gn. Gn. Gn. darbenebenst hertzlich wünschende, der Allerhöchste
wolle E. E. E. Gn. Gn. Gn. bey guter beharrlicher Gesundheit, glük-

ship. And this was in the following way: First, the firm conclusion is made that no one, whoever he may be, is without Christ Jesus as a right true friend to whom one can securely flee in a thousand anguishes and soul's needs. In further confirmation of this, his other friends — the devil, the world, and human flesh and blood — would immediately after this [i.e., after the person's turning to Christ] pull off their deceitful masks with which they intend to lead people astray in the name of friendship. So that the grandeur of this spiritual soulfriendship may be illuminated somewhat we have set forth as the fifth consideration, who our soulfriend is, namely, Christ Jesus the true substantial God from everlasting to everlasting. In the sixth consideration, we have however shown who we, in contrast, are, namely, poor, miserable, mortal people who with our sins have deserved God's wrath and disgrace, temporal death and eternal damnation. So that one may also know how one can come to such spiritual soulfriendship, we have shown the means in the following considerations, namely, devout listening to the divine Word, use of the holy sacraments, and true, soul-strengthening faith. Finally, there follows[4] the excellent benefit that this spiritual soulfriendship brings with it. The teaching poetry that is intermixed is in part taken from holy Scripture, in part from the Fathers and other authors, in part written by ourselves. Yet this is to be remembered about this and about the emblems, that they should not be interpreted further than their own set limits allow, for otherwise ideas which don't fit will result. Concerning the fathers and other authors whom we often quote here: Of course, we freely confess that we ourselves have not read them altogether thoroughly. Nevertheless we have had some opportunities to hand [to read them] so that the most important things from them are known to us to some degree. And we would humbly and obediently submit even this little book to E. E. E. Gn. Gn. Gn., in consideration that next to God we have no one on earth more to thank or to whom we are more indebted than E. E. E. Gn. Gn. Gn. Besides that, we sincerely wish the All-highest would uphold E. E. E. Gn. Gn. Gn. in persistent good health, good fortune, and a peaceful reign, keeping [you] in a

und friedlicher Regierung, und bey allen hohen selbst verlangten Chur-
und Fürstlichen Wohlergehen noch viel lange Zeit väterlich
aufbehalten, vor allem Ubel mächtiglich beschützen, und mit
himlischen Segen reichlich überschütten, zu welchem Ende E. E. E.
Gn. Gn. Gn. wir hiermit der Göttlichen Macht-Schirmung
gehorsamlich übertragen allstets verbleibende
E. E. E. G. G. G.
Demühtig-gehorsamste
Enkelin Tochter und
Dienerin
Anna Sophia Landgräfin zu Hessen, Pröbstin

Anhang etlicher anderen geistlichen Betrachtungen, Worinnen erkläret
wird, was einem iedwedern Christen, insondenheit aber dem
Frauenzimmer stets zu beobachten und zu verrichten wohl anstehe.

Bißhero haben wir dir, Christliebendes Gemühte, die treue Seelen-
Freundschaft deines Heilandes Christi Jesu, welche er gegen dir
iederzeit träget, wie auch die Mittel in solche Freundschaft zu gelangen,
fürgezeiget, und zwar nach dem Maß der Weisheit, welche uns GOtt
aus Gnaden hierzu verliehen hat. Verhoffentlich wird dir diese unsere
wohlmeinende Arbeit, wo nicht belieblich, doch zum wenigsten nicht
verächtlich fallen. Findest du etwas gutes darinnen, so schreibe es
einig und allein dem Göttlichen Beystande des heiligen Geistes zu,
als welchem ich es auch selbsten einig und alleine zuschreibe, und für
welchem ich meinem JEsu demühtig dancke. Findest du aber etwas
mangelhaftes darinnen, so rechne es mir und meiner Schwachheit
zu. Damit ich mich aber noch ferner ümb dich, Christliebendes
Gemühte, möge bedienet machen, so wil ich dir anißo, zu förderst zu
GOttes Ehren, und dann zu deiner Seelen Nutzen, in etlich wenig
Betrachtungen fürstellen, was einem iedweden Christen, insonderheit
aber dem Frauenzimmer stets zu beobachten und zu verrichten wohl
anstehe.

Von denen Kloster-Jungfern der heidnischen Göttin Vesta, schreibet
Lipsius, daß ihre Verrichtungen absonderlich in diesen dreyen
bestanden: in Wachen, in Aufsicht haben, und in Opffern. Wachen
musten sie bey Tag und Nacht, damit das Feuer, welches der Vesta zu
Ehren unablässig erhalten werden muste, nicht ausleschen möchte.
Aufsicht musten sie haben auf das Bild der Palladis, auf welchem der

fatherly way in all the high electoral and princely prosperity that you desire for a long time more, protect [you] powerfully from all evil and shower [you] with heavenly riches. To which end, E. E. E. Gn. Gn. Gn., we herewith remain always obediently given over to the divine shield of power.

E. E. E. G. G. G.

Humbly obedient

granddaughter, daughter, and

servant,

Anna Sophia, Countess of Hesse/Pröbstin

Appendix of several other spiritual considerations wherein will be explained what every Christian, but especially women, constantly needs to observe and perform.

Until now we have shown you, Christ-loving soul, the true soulfriendship of your Savior Christ Jesus that he shows to you every time, along with the means to arrive at such friendship. And this [we have done] according to the measure of wisdom that God out of grace has bestowed on us. Hopefully where our well-intended work, if not pleasing to you, will at least not appear to be contemptible. If you find something good in it, then attribute it completely and solely to the divine assistance of the Holy Spirit to whom I also completely and solely attribute it, and for which I humbly thank my Jesus. If you also find some imperfections in it, attribute these to me and my weakness. So that I may further serve you, Christ-loving soul, I will put forward several small considerations — to honor God and for your soul's use — that every Christian, but especially women, does well to observe and practice.

Regarding the cloistered maidens of the heathen goddess Vesta, Lipsius[5] wrote that their duties consisted especially in these three: in watching, in taking care, and in sacrificing. They must watch by day and night so that the fire which must constantly be preserved to honor Vesta might not burn out. They must take care of the picture of Palladis, upon which the city's welfare was based as they imagined, so

Stadt Heil beruhete, wie sie sich einbildeten, damit solches nicht
verlohren würde, oder sonsten Schaden litte. Opffern musten sie,
und zwar solches auch bey Tag und bey Nacht unaufhörlich.
Was diese aus Aberglauben der Vesta zu Ehren gethan haben, das
lasset uns aus rechtschaffenen Glauben unserm JEsu zu Ehren auch
thun. Anfänglich lasset uns wachen, und zwar erstlich in steter
Bußfertigkeit. Zwar es heisset in gemein, interdum bonus etiam. . . .
dormitat Homerus, vornehme Leute schlaffen auch, das ist, heilige
Leute. Ja die aller heiligsten Leute fehlen und sündigen auch. Petrus
und die andern Apostel, welche mit an dem Oelberge wahren,
schlaffen auch, und zwar so gar, daß sie der HErr JEsus fragen muß:
Könnet ihr denn nicht eine Stunde mit mir wachen? Seid ihr denn
so gar verschlaffen? Ist es euch denn unmöglich eine Stunde mit mir
zu wachen? Ach freylich! liebster JEsu, freylich, freylich, können wir
nicht eine Stunde ungeschlaffen hinbringen, unsere Schwachheit ist
so groß daß nicht eine Stunde fürüber gehet, da wir nicht ein
Sündenschläfflein thun, wo nicht allezeit eusserlich, dennoch
innerlich mit unsern Gedancken und Begierden. Clemens
Alexandrinus nennet den Schlaf einen Zöllner, wenn er saget,
Somnus non secus ac publicanus dimidium vitæ tempus nobiscum
dividit. . . .
Das andere Ampt der Vestalischen Kloster-Jungfrauen bestunde
darinnen, daß sie musten Acht haben auf das Palladium, oder Bildnus
der heidnischen Göttin Pallas, damit solches nicht irgends verlohren
würde, oder sonsten einigen Schaden litte. Denn wie sie darfür hielten,
so solte auf demselbigen Bilde des gantzen gemeinen Wesens
Wohlfahrt bestehen. Wir haben auch ein herrliches Palladium, darauf
nicht nur unser zeitliches Wohlergehen, sondern unserer Seelen Heil
und Selligkeit beruhet. Wust du wissen, was es ist? Es ist Gottes Wort,
Gottes Wort ist es. O das ist ein herrlicher Schatz, den wir wohl in
Acht nehmen müssen. Diesen Schatz befiehlet uns Gott der HErr
auf das allergetreulichste. Deut. 6. v. 6.8. Die Wort die ich dir heute
gebiete, soltu zu Hertzen nehmen, und solt sie binden zum Zeichen auf
deine Hand, und sollen dir ein Denckmahl seyn für deinen Augen. . . .
Das dritte Ampt der Vestalischen Kloster-Jungfrauen war, daß sie
stets opffern musten. Wiewohl wir Christen nun zwar heutiges Tages
keine leibliche Opffer zu bringen von Nöhten haben, sintemal unser
JEsus mit einem Opffer vollendet hat in Ewigkeit, die geheiliget

that it would not be lost or otherwise suffer damage. They must also sacrifice without ceasing by day and by night.

What these out of superstition have done to honor Vesta, that let us also do, out of rightly created faith, to honor our Jesus.

To begin, let us watch, primarily in constant penitential readiness. It is true that normally "sometimes even good . . . Homer sleeps," that noble people also sleep, that is, holy people. Yes, the holiest people fail and also sin. Peter and the other Apostles who were on the Mount of Olives also slept, so deeply that the Lord Jesus actually had to ask them: Can you not watch with me for an hour? Are you sleeping so soundly? Is it then impossible for you to watch with me for one hour? O, so true! dearest Jesus, so true, so true that we cannot bring forth a wakeful hour. Our weakness is so great that not an hour goes by that we do not take a little sleep of sin; if not always openly then internally with our thoughts and desires. Clement of Alexandria called this sleep a "tax-collector" when he said: "Sleep is not fruitful, a tax collector that divides and separates a measure of life from time.". . .

The second office of the Vestal virgins consists in having to take care of the Palladium (or a portrait of the heathen goddess, Pallas) so that it would not be lost or suffer damage. They held then that the prosperity of the entire community exists in this same picture. We also have a glorious Palladium, not only our earthly welfare but based upon our soul's health and salvation. Do you know what it is? It is God's Word; God's Word it is. O, that is a splendid treasure of which we must fully take care! God the Lord commended this treasure to us in the very truthful Deuteronomy 6:6, 8: "Take to heart the Word that I enjoin you today. It should bind to your hand as a sign and should be a monument for your eyes." . . .

The third office of the Vestal Virgins was that they must always sacrifice. These days, it is true that we Christians have no need to bring bodily sacrifices since with one sacrifice our Jesus has accomplished eternal salvation, as the Apostle Paul said, Hebrews 10:14. O!

werden, wie der Apostel Paulus saget Ebr. 10.v.14. Ach! wenn sich
Jesus für uns nicht aufgeopffert hätte, so wären alle Opffer viel zu
wenig gewesen, uns von einiger Sünde zu erlösen. Alles Bocksblut,
aller Kälber Blut, ja aller Menschen Blut wäre nicht kräftig gewesen,
für eine einige sünde gnug zu thun, wo nicht Jesus durch sein eigen
Blut in das Heilige eingegangen hätte. Ebr. 9/12. Je dennoch sollen
rechtschaffene Christen auch täglich ihr Opffer bringen für Gottes
Angesicht, Denn wir sind allesampt geistliche Priester, Christus Jesus
hat uns geliebet und gewaschen von der Sünden mit seinem Blute,
und hat uns zu Königen und Priestern gemachet für Gott und seinem
Vater. Apoc. 1. v. 8. Derowegen so müssen wir auch als geistliche
Priester unsere geistliche Opffer bringen. . . .

if Jesus had not offered himself up for us, all sacrifices would be too little to deliver us from a single sin. All goat's blood, all calf's blood, yes, all human blood would not be powerful enough to make up for a single sin, had Jesus not entered into holiness through his own blood (Heb. 9:12). Nevertheless justified Christians should also daily bring their sacrifice to God's sight because we are all similarly spiritual priests. Christ Jesus has loved us and washed us of our sins with his blood, and has made us kings and priests for God and his Father (Rev. 1:8). Because of that, we must also bring our spiritual sacrifice as spiritual priests. . . .

Notes

1. This is an abbreviation for the titles of honor for Sophia's parents and grandmother, to whom this work was addressed. She uses this when she is addressing them directly; it might best be translated "your graces."
2. Anna Maria von Schurman (1607-1678) was a Dutch woman widely regarded as the most learned woman of her day in Europe. She learned many ancient and modern languages and wrote a number of works. Her best-known work, to which Sophia is here referring, was a treatise which she wrote originally in Latin debating the question "whether the study of letters is fitting to a Christian woman." This was translated into many languages, including an English version in 1659 which had the title *The Learned Maid, or Whether a Maid may be called a Scholar.*
3. There is a marginal note here: August de S. Virgin. Cap 27. For clarity, Augustine's text is put in quotation marks, with Sophia Eleonora's paraphrased translation following each phrase. Her citations are very accurate to the *De sancta virginitate* text.
4. A section given over to contemplative verses with illustrations follows the body of this letter. It is not included in this translation. The "emblems" referred to in the following sentence are these illustrations.
5. Justus Lipsius (1547-1606) was a Flemish scholar of Roman literature who edited many works of Latin literature and wrote extensively on Roman religion and philosophy. The vestal virgins, who Sophia is discussing here, were six women in ancient Rome chosen to maintain the sacred fire of the goddess Vesta, which was never to be allowed to go out.

Martha Elisabeth Zitter

Gründliche Ursachen welche Jungfer Marthen Elisabeth Zitterin bewogen, das Frantzöische alias Weiß-Frauen Kloster in Erffurt, Ursuliner Ordens zuverlassen und sich zu der waaren Evangelischen Religion zu bekennen

Martha Elisabeth Zitter

Basic reasons which have induced the maiden Martha Elisabeth Zitter to leave the French or white-ladies convent of the Ursuline order in Erfurt and to profess the true evangelical religion.

Martha Elisabeth Zitter

Gründliche Ursachen welche Jungfer Marthen Elisabeth Zitterin bewogen, das Frantzöische alias Weiß-Frauen Kloster in Erffurt, Ursuliner Ordens zuverlassen und sich zu der waaren Evangelischen Religion zu bekennen

In einen Schreiben an ihre Mutter, Frau Maria Margaretha, jetzo Herrn Johan Hübners von Rosenberg, Obr-Leutenants und Fürstl. Bamberg. Commendantes in Cronach Eheliebste.

Angezeiget und zu Abwendung ungleicher Nachrede zum viertenmal gedruckt in Jena, 1678

Hochgeehrte und Hertzliebste Frau Mutter.

Das sich dieselbe über die Zeitung meines Außtrits aus dem Kloster und der aus ohnzweyfelichem Eingeben des H. Geistes geschenenen Aenderung der Päbstischen Religion sehr betrübet und hefftig geeysert, befrembdet mich umb deßwillen mit nichten, weil mir nicht unbekant, daß sie aller Wissenschaft ermangelt, was in sich begreift die Evangelische Relgion darzu. Ich mich anietzo aus einer particular Gnade Gottes, so wol mit dem Hertzen als dem Munde, mit danckbarem Gemüthe gegen seine Göttliche Majestät bekenne. Damit Sie sich aber hierunter desto besser beruhigen könne, erkenne Ich mich verpflichtet, Ihr die motiven anzuzeigen, so ich gehabt, so wol den Orden als die Religion solcher Gestalt zuverlassen. Was nun angehet den dem Namen, aber dem Werck nach, Geistlichen Stand, so ist der Frau Mutter schon zu vor wol bekant, daß ich in denselben nicht auß freyer Wahl getreten, sondern von Ihr vor nunmehro 8. Jahren in dem vierzehenden Jahre meines Alters, zu dem Ende in das Kloster geschicket worden bin, die Frantzöische Sprache und allerhand der Jungfräulichen Tugend wol anständige Arbeit darinne zu erlernen. Als ich aber kaum hatte angefangen, darinnen etwas bekant zu werden, und noch kein Monat vorbey gegangen war, fingen etliche von den Ursuliner Nonnen an, ihrer Art nach, mich durch allerhand Mittel und Wege dahin zuvermögen, daß ich ihren Habit anlegen möchte. Ob ich nun wol wie ich mit GOtt bezeugen kan, den höchsten Widerstand in meinem Gemüthe darüber empfand, ließ ich mich doch endlich in meinem dazumal unverständigen Jahren bethören,

Martha Elisabeth Zitter

Basic reasons which have induced the maiden Martha Elisabeth Zitter[1] to leave the French or white-ladies convent of the Ursuline order in Erfurt and to profess the true evangelical religion.

In a letter to her mother Mrs. Maria Margaretha, now the wife of Mr. Johann Hubner from Rosenberg, over-lieutenant and commander in Cronach for the prince of Bamberg.

Announced and printed for the fourth time to avert much slander in Jena, 1678

High honorable and beloved mother,

[I know] that you were very afflicted by and spoke strongly about the news of my leaving the convent and changing from the papist religion — which happened through the undoubted prompting of the Holy Spirit — and that you disinherited me with nothing because of this. It is not unknown to me that you lack all knowledge of what the evangelical religion understands itself to be, which I now profess out of the particular grace of God with both my heart and mouth with a thankful soul toward his godly majesty. So that you will be able henceforth to calm yourself down better, I realize I am obligated to indicate the reasons that I had to leave the order and this form of religion. That which goes by the name — but not the deed — of the spiritual estate is already known to [you] my mother. [You know] that I did not enter into this of free choice, but was sent into the convent by you eight years ago when I was fourteen years old, in order to learn the French language and all sorts of maidenly virtues as well as respectable work. Very shortly after I had begun to become somewhat comfortable with such things, and not yet a month had gone by, some of the Ursuline nuns began to try to influence me through all types of means and ways to want to put on their habit. Although I — as God can attest — felt the strongest opposition in my soul to this, I finally let myself — at that time [I was] still foolish

und gab das Ja-Wort von mir, der Hoffnung daß nach verflossener
Prob-Zeit ich füglicher Ursach haben würde, der überlästigen persuasion der Ursuliner mich zu entbrechen. Was für List sie aber
dargegen gebraucht ist der Frau Mutter nich unbekant. Denn sie
haben mir, ihrer eigenen Ordens-Regel zu wider, welche zum
wenigsten drey Monate zwischen dem Eingange ins Novitiat und
Anlegung des Habits erfordert, nach 14. Tagen meines Eingangs ins
Novitiat den Ordens-Habit angeleget, und zwar ohn eintzige
Erklärung der Regel und Ordens-Gebräuche, auch mit höchsten
Widerwillen und Mißfallen der Fr. Mutter, welche durchaus und
auff keinerley Manier dahin konte persuadiret werden, darein zu
consentiren, welches Ich mir auch, wie meine kindlich Schuldigkeit
erforderte, tieff zu Gemüth fassete. Aber es wurde alles in geschwinder
Eyle zu Anlegung des Habits bereitet, daß ich mich ferner nicht
darwider setzen konte, in dem mir die Ursuliner so viel vorschwätzeten
daß Ich ihnen bey damahligem Alter darauff mit Gegenantwort nicht
zu begegnen wuste. Unter andern weiß ich mich noch wohl zu
erinnern, daß mir ein Jesuit sehr eyfrig zuredete, und vorgab: Wenn
gleich der Vater blutige Zähren weinend vor der Thür-Schwellen
legen, und die Mutter mit Ausrauffung aller Haare todt zu der Erden
niedersüncke, so solte man über den Vater hinschreiten, die Mutter
liegen lassen, und ins Kloster lauffen. Wie conform aber dieses dem
vierdten Gebote Gottes sey, kan mit mir ein jeglicher Verständiger
erachten. Ich erinnene mich hierbey indessen, was ich ohnlängst
gelesen habe beym Evangelisten Marco am 7. Als v. 5. die Phariseer
zu unserm Heylande sageten: Warum wandeln deine Jünger nich
nach den Auffsätzen der Eltesten? gab er ihnen v. 6. biß 13. diese
Antwort: Wol fein hat von euch Jesaias geweissaget, wie geschrieben
stehet: Diß Volck ehret mich mit den Lippen, aber ihr Hertz ist fern
von mir. Vergeblich aber ists, daß sie mir dienen, dieweil sie lehren
solche Lehre, die nichts ist den Menschen Gebot. Ihr verlasset
Gottes Gebot und haltet der Menschen Auffsätze von Krügen und
Trinck-Gefässen zuwaschen und dergleichen thut ihr viel. Und
Er sprach zu ihnen: Wol fein habt ihr Gottes Gebot auffgehaben
auff daß ihr eure Auffsätze haltet. Denn Moses hat gesagt: Du solt
deinen Vater und deine Mutter ehren, und wer Vater und Mutter
flucht, der sol des Todes sterben: Ihr aber lehret, wenn einer spricht
zum Vater oder Mutter: Corban: daß ist: wenn ichs opffere: so ist
dirs viel nützer, der thut wol. Und so lasset ihr hinfort ihn nichts

— be persuaded, and said yes, with the hope that after the trial-period had passed I would have appropriate reasons to break myself off from the overburdened ways of the Ursulines. What types of tricks they used against this are not unknown to [you] my mother. Contrary to the rules of their own order — which demand at least three months between beginning a novitiate and putting on a habit — they put a habit on me fourteen days after I began my novitiate. This was without any explanation of the rules and customs of the order and with the greatest reluctance and displeasure of the abbess, who could in no way be persuaded to consent at all to this, which I also took deep into my heart, as my childlike obligations demanded. But everything was prepared in greatest haste for putting on the habit, so that I could not set myself against this. The Ursulines chattered so much to me about this, that I — at that age — did not know how to meet them with a rejoinder. Among other things, I can still remember well that a Jesuit spoke to me very energetically and said: "Even if your father lies crying with bloody tears in front of the door sill, and your mother sinks dead to the ground pulling out all her hair, you should still step over your father and let your mother lie in order to run into the convent." Every reasonable person can consider with me how much this does not fit with the fourth commandment. I remember in regard to this what I read long ago in the seventh [chapter] of the Gospel of Mark. As the Pharisees said to our Saviour in verse five: "Why don't your disciples follow the writings of the elders?" He gave them this answer in verses six through thirteen: "Isaiah has prophesied well, as it is written: 'These people honor me with their lips, but their hearts are far from me. You serve me in vain because the lessons that you teach are nothing more than human rules.' You forsake God's commandments and hold to human compositions about washing mugs and drinking-glasses, and such things you do a lot." And he said to them: "You have certainly broken God's commandment in that you follow your own compositions, for Moses said, 'You should honor your father and your mother, and whoever flees from father and mother shall die.' You, however, teach that when one speaks to one's father or mother [one should say] Corban,[2] that is, I offered it [to God]; this is much more useful to you and you do well. So from now on you let no one do anything for their father or

thun seinem Vater odern seiner Mutter. Und hebet auff Gottes Wort durch eure Auffsätze die ihr auffgesetzt habt, und deßgleichen thut ihr viel.

Sie pflegen zwar außzugeben: Wir bereden niemand zum Geistlichen Stand, es geschiehet aus eines jedenfreywilliger Wahl: Aber Ich kans bezeugen, und mit mir noch viele andere, aus was für freyer Wahl wir in den Orden getreten und folgends Profes gethan haben. Daß Ich dieselbe mehr aus Zwang als freyer Wahl gethan habe, bekräfftigen nebst vielen andern Anzeigungen auch die grossen difficultäten die Ich unter wehrenden Prob-Jahren nach Anlegung des Habits gehabt u. öffendlich erkläret habe, darüber auch die F. Mutter mit grossen Freude in Erffurth gereiset mich von dannen wieder mit sich nach Hause zuführen, wornach ich dann selbst hertzlich verlanget. Daß aber mit ihrer höchten Betrübniß mein Außgang seinen erwüntschten Fortgang nich gehabt, kam ebener massen her aus einer verführischen Persuasion Herrn. P. Marcus Schönemanns, unsers Klosters Beicht Vatters, wie auch die Ursulinen Nonnen, welche betheuerlich versprachen, mich jederzeit, wann ich es verlangen würde, ohne einige Hindernis in ein ander Kloster darinnen Ich mehrere satisfaction haben könte zulassen, darbey sie mich dann so viel eher gewinnen und einnehmen konten, weil meine difficultäten nicht bestunden in Bereuung des Verlassenen oder sonst einigen zeitlichen motiven, sondern allein in dem, daß das übelführende Klosterleben klar widerspricht der guten opinion, so man von demselben hat. Denn die bösen Exempel, dergleichen ich in keiner Privat Behausung ausser dem Kloster jemaln gesehen, machten mir den Orden und Nonnen-Stand täglich mehr verächtlich.

Und wie konte es anders seyn? Wann man sein Gemüth ein wenig erhebet, und etwas eigentlicher betrachtet, worinnen sie stellen die Heiligkeit, die Erwartung grosser Belohnung und hohen Ruhm der Vollkommenheit, so sie für andern Christlichen Seelen haben wollen. So viel als ich gesehen und außdrücklich weiß, so bestehet es darinne, daß sie gewisse Stunden im Chore ihre horas in Lateinischer Sprache auff der Post herschwätzen, welche sie doch nicht verstehen. Was nun für Auffmercksamkeit, Andacht und Trost sich darbey befinde, ist leichtlich zu erachten. Ferner bestehe es in dem, daß sie sich alle Wochen einmal selbst Blutdrünstig geisseln, silberne Spörnlein und Messingene Gürtel mit Stacheln wie auch von Pferde Haaren an dem blossen Leibe tragen: eine umb die andere die von denen über Tisch sitzenden

mother. And you annul God's Word with the compositions you have set down, and you do this a lot."

They take care to give out, "We never persuade anyone to join a religious order; it always happens through free choice." But I can testify — and with me many others — with what kind of free choice we came into the order and afterwards made our profession. Along with other indications, the many difficulties that I had and publicly spoke about during my probation years after putting on the habit indicate that I did this more from coercion than free choice. Because of this, the abbess travelled with great joy to Erfurt in order to take me home again with her, which I had heartily requested. [The fact] that — with great grief — my desired departure did not proceed, can be attributed equally to the enticing persuasion of Pastor Marcus Schönemann, our convent's confessor, and the Ursuline nuns who solemnly promised that any time I requested it, they would let me go to another convent where I would be more satisfied without any hindrance. With this they won me over and took me in more easily, for my difficulties did not consist in contact with those who had left or other temporal motives, but alone in the fact that convent life was being led in a bad way, which clearly contradicted the good opinion that one had of it. For the bad examples, the like of which I had never seen in a private house outside of the convent, made the order and the nuns' existence more contemptible to me every day.

And how could it be otherwise? If one puts one's mind to it a little, one can actually observe, though what [actions] they think they have greater holiness, expectations of rewards, and high fame of perfection than other Christian souls. As much as I have seen and know for sure, this consists of chattering the monastic hours in Latin at certain times in the choir, which they don't understand. It is easy to see what sort of attention, devotion and comfort will be found in this. Further, this [holiness] consists of: whipping themselves once a week until the blood flows; wearing little silver barbs, brass belts with points, and horsehair belts on their bare bodies; eating food — which they have begged from the nuns who sit at the table — from off of the floor in the

Nonnen erbettelte Speisen auff dem Erdboden in aller Gegenwart geniessen; grosse höltzerne Creutze mit Stricken herum tragen; sich vor der andern Füsse werffen, und dieselbe küssen; auf dem Erdboden liegend mit ausgestreckten Armen beten; Ihre Verbrechen alle Sonnabende des Morgens in Gegenwart der gantzen Communität kniend der Oberen oder Würdigen Mutter und des Nachmittags dem Confessori in gehiem bekennen; bißweilen in Wasser und Brot fasten; bißweilen auch härene Kleider auff blossen Leib ziehen und dergleichen Menschen Gedichte mehr sind, darauff sie, wie gedacht, alle ihre vermeynte Heiligkeit stellen.

Hierzu gehören auch die Gelübde der Armut, Keuschheit, und Gehorsams, die aber eben so gering zu schätzen als die vorhergehenden Menschen Satzungen (1.) weil dieselbe in GOttes Wort Neues und Altes Testaments nirgends fürgeschrieben noch weniger geboten und befohlen sind. Hätte solcher Stand GOtt für andern gefallen, so würde gewiß der Sohn des ewigen Vaters nicht unterlassen haben, darvon einigen Befehl zugeben, ja Satz- und Ordnungen nach welchen derselbe zuführen vorschreiben lassen? (2.) Weil sie nicht die conditiones haben, die zu einem rechten Gelübde erfordert werden. Und zwar 1. daß sie allein Gott den Herren geschehen sollen, weil die Geistlichen Gelübde ins gemein sind ein Stück der Bekäntnis des Glaubens und der Anruffung so allein GOtt gebühret. Nun thun sie aber dieselbe nicht allein Gott, sondern auch der Heiligen Mutter GOttes Marien und den Ordens-Stifftern und Patronen. 2. Das Geloben muß geschehen aus freyem vollkommenen Willen und wolbedachtem Vorsatz. Daß aber dieses bey den Kloster-Gelübden nicht beobachtet werde, brauchet keines Beweises. Die Exempel bekräfftigen es klar, welche ich so wol an mir selbst, als an andern habe erfahren, daß die meisten, sonderlich von der Jungfräulichen Jugend in ihren unverständigen Jahren, theils von ihren Beicht-Vätern ausserhalb der Klöster, mehrentheils aber in Klöstern beredet und gezwungen werden, in solchen Stand sich zu verloben, offtermals mit höchstem Mißfallen und Widerwillen der Eltern. Worauß denn erfolget der 3. Abgang derer zu einem Gelübd gehörigen conditionen, nemlich, daß dasselbe müste geschenen von Personen, die ihrer selbst mächtig und in keiner Eltern Gewalt mehr sind. Nun ist aber gewiß, daß eine Jungfrau von 14. 15. oder 16. Jahren ihrer noch nicht mächtig ist, sondern den Eltern aus der Macht so sie über dieselbe haben, verführet und entführet werde. (3.) befindet sich auch kein bewerthes Exempel

presence of all; carrying around large wooden crosses with ropes; throwing themselves before the feet of others and kissing them; lying on the floor with arms outstretched praying; confessing their sins every Saturday, in the morning kneeling in the presence of the abbess or reverend mother and the whole community and in the afternoon in secret to the confesssor; sometimes fasting on bread and water; sometimes wearing hair shirts on their bare bodies; and other similar human inventions in which they — as noted — place all of their supposed holiness.

The vows of poverty, chastity, and obedience also belong here, which should be valued just as little as the previously noted human rules, (1) for they are established nowhere in the Old or New Testament of God's Word nor are they commanded or recommended. If such a state [i.e., being a member of a religious order] had pleased God more than others, would the son of the heavenly father have neglected to give any recommendations about this, or even to prescribe the rules and ordinances for following this? (2) They don't have the conditions that are necessary for a true vow. These are (a) that they should be given to God the Lord alone, because spiritual vows are all a part of the confession of faith and the witness that is due to God alone. But they make these not only to God, but also to the holy mother of God, Mary, and to the order's founders and patrons. (b) The vow must proceed completely from free will and a well-thought-out sense of purpose. No proof is needed that this is not seen in convent vows. The examples, which I myself and others have experienced, clearly support this. Most [girls], while still in their maidenly youth and foolish years, were persuaded and forced by their confessors outside of the convent or even more by those in the convent to promise [to join] the order. [This was] often with the highest displeasure and opposition of their parents. From this follows the third [point]: (c) Their departure to a condition bound by an oath. That is, this may only happen when persons are independent and are not under their parents' authority. Now it is certain that a young woman of 14, 15, or 16 is not yet independent, but has been led astray and abducted from the authority of her parents. (3) There is no worthy example in Holy

in der H. Schrifft und der ersten reinen Christlichen Kirchen derer die die Kloster Gelübde auf solche Art, wie sie anitzo gethan werden, geleistet und gehalten. Sie geloben Armuth, nicht daß sie willens sind, Armuth zu leyden, sondern sie begeben sich allein ihrer zeitlichen Güter derselben im Kloster ohne grosse Müh und Kummer zu geniessen. Wie denn auch warhafftig geschiehet, daß die meisten bey ihren gethanen Gelübden der Armuth in Klöstern mehr Bequemligkeiten bekommen, als sie sonst ausser denselben würden gehabt haben. Sagen sie das Gelübde der Armuth bestehe fürnehmlich darinne, daß man das Hertz von dem zeitlichen Gut abziehe, so ist zuvor schon ausgemacht daß solch Gelübde krafft ihrer Tauff-und Christen-Pflicht alle Christen zu observiren und das Hertz an Gott und nicht an zeitliche Güter zu hengen schuldig sind. Ich könte noch ein mehrers aus eigener Erfahrung von solchen unförmlichen Gelübde der Armuth anführen, welches ich aber, weil ich dergleichen in der Evangelischen Lehrer Büchern schon ausgeführet gesehen zu Vermeydung Weitläufftigkeit unterlasse.

Was das ander Gelübde der Keuschheit oder Ehe-Verschwerung anlanget, davon stehet meinem Jungfräulichen Stande viel zu schreiben nicht an.

Das dritte Gelübde des gehorsams aber begreiffet ein so lächerliches Wesen in sich als die anderen. Durch dasselbe verbinden sie sich, einer gewissen Oberin in allen Sachen blind hin zu gehorsamen, welches ja klar wider die Schriffte ist, als welche befihlet Act. 5. v. 29 Mann müsse GOTT mehr gehorchen als den Menschen. Daß aber zum öfftern die Befehle der Ordens-Oberen wider GOtt und seine heilige Gebote lauffen, könte ich mit vielen bewusten Exempeln beweisen. Unter vielen wil ich nur ein eintziges anführen und fragen: Ob es den Geboten GOttes gemäß sey, wann die Oberin einer ihrer untergebenen Nonnen befihlet, von einer andern der sie nicht geneiget ist, erdichtete Unwarheiten, als gründliche Warheiten auffzubringen und die Unschuldige damit zu beschuldigen, einer andern aber aufferleget, daß sie der jenigen, welche solche Verleumbdung erst angebracht, beyfallen, und durch ihr falsch Zeugniß die Unschuldige soll helffen zur Straffe verdammen? Dergleichen Befehle offtermahls in dem Kloster, aus welchem mich die Göttliche Güte auff sonderbahre Weise ausgeführet hat, geschehen sind, wie mit mir auff beschehene Nachfrage werden bezeugen können die jenigen Christlichen Hertzen und auffrichtigen Seelen, die durch dergleichen Verleumbdungen

Scripture or the first pure Christian churches, where such convent vows as they are now performed were sworn or upheld. They swear to poverty, not because they are willing to suffer poverty, but because they give up their worldly goods [knowing] they will enjoy the same in the convent without trouble or worry. It also truly happens that, with their vow of poverty, most of them receive more comforts in the convent than they would have had outside. They say that the vow of poverty consists primarily in pulling one's heart away from worldly goods, but this has already been agreed to, for all Christians are responsible to observe such a vow because of their baptismal and Christian duties to hang their hearts on God and not on worldly goods. I would certainly add many things from my own experience about such unwieldy vows of poverty, but I have seen these detailed often in the books for evangelical teachers, so in order to avoid too many details I will omit them.

Things which concern the second vow of chastity or celibacy are not appropriate for me to write about, given my maidenly state.

The third vow of obedience, however, includes something just as ridiculous as the second [vow]. Through this vow they bind themselves in blind obedience to a certain leader, which is clearly against Scripture, as it states in Acts 5: 29 that one must obey God more than people. The commands of the leaders of the order often run contrary to God and his holy commandments, which I can demonstrate with many examples. Among the many I will only cite a single one, and ask: Whether it is in accordance with the will of God, when the mother superior commands one of the nuns that is under her authority to bring forth invented truths as if they were truths about another [nun], towards whom she is not well disposed, in order to accuse an innocent [person]? And imposes on another, that she support the one who first brought up the slander, and help damn the innocent to punishment through false witness? Commands like this happened often in the convent, which God's goodness has led me out of in strange ways. Those Christian hearts and sincere souls who were often painfully punished through such slanders can testify to this upon

öffters schmertzliche sind gezüchtiget worden, welchen Ich von Grund meines Hertzens von dem barmhertzigen GOtt wünsche gleichmässige Erleuchtung, wie wir widerfahren und Mittel sich so wol mit ihren durch Christi Blut theuer erkaufften Seelen, als den Leiberen aus der Barbarischen Tyranney des D. Hunolts und der Frantzöischen Nonnen in Erfffurt zu erretten, und an einen solchen Ort zu gelangen, wo sie sich durch treuen Unterricht aus GOttes Wort und gute Exempel Evangelischer rechtschaffener Christen mit mir erbauen und trösten können. Dann mir nur allzuwohl bewust ist, wie sehr es schmertzet, wann man im benanten Kloster sehen und erfahren muß, wie da regieret Hochmut u. Ehrgeitz, Neid, Verleumbdung, Zorn, Unwarheit, Unbilligkeit, und andere Tod-Sunden.

Ich setze mit Bedacht den Hochmut und Ehrgeitz oben an: dann aus denselben entspringen alle die anderen. Der Hochmut und Hoffarth der ietzo noch vorhandenen vier Aeltesten machet daß, ob sie wol sonst wann es zum Schaden der anderen Jüngeren gereichet, sehr einträchtig sind, dannoch, weil keine der andern den Vorzug in Aemptern gönnet, sie so verhaßt und verbittert auff einander sind, daß sie so gar mit Entäusserung der Hertzen, auch die Entäusserung der Conversation und Wohnung suchen. Ja es ist wol ein halb Jahr hingegangen, daß sie nicht zusammen kommen sind, nichts als stachelicht- und zänckische Wort gegen einander, bey anderen mit beyden Theilen uninteressirten aber eine von der andern sehr ärgerliche Sachen geredet, und ob wol dieselbe, weil es die Wercke selbst ausgewiesen, in der Warheit betanden, so erscheinet doch daraus, wie weit die Regiersucht eine und die ander getrieben hat. Es war ihnen nicht gnug, daß eine Parthey die andere durch Entdeckung ihres Gottlosen Lebens im Kloster verachtet machete, sondern sie bemüheten sich ängstiglich, in andere Klöster so wohl als nach Maintz an Ihre Churfl. Gnd. solch Brieffe zu schrieben, dadurch dieselbe gemüssiget worden drey von Erffurt wider in ihr fast auf die hundert Meilen darvon entlegenes Kloster zu verschicken. Daß aber solches Fortschickung der einen damahligen Parthey der übrigen ietzo noch regierenden vieren Hochmut und Ehrgeitz gleichwohl nicht niederlegen oder abwenden können, bezeugen die listig erfundene Mittel und Verleumbdungen mit welchen sie die jenigen von ihnen, welche sie vermuthen, daß sie den Vorzug vor den andern erlangen möchten, bey der höchsten Obrigkeit und anderen, welche sie vermeinen, daß sie etwas darbey thun können, verkleinern, veracht-

request. From the bottom of my heart, I wish them the same enlightenment of the merciful God as I experienced, and the same means to save themselves — with both their souls, which have been bought through the dear blood of Christ, and their bodies — from the barbarous tyranny of Dr. Hunolt and the French nuns in Erfurt. And [I wish] that they would come to such a place where they could edify and console themselves with me through true teaching from God's Word and the good example of righteous evangelical Christians. For I know only too well, how much it hurts when one must see and experience in the aforementioned convent, how pride and ambition, envy, slander, anger, untruth, unfairness and other deadly sins reign there.

I deliberately began above with pride and ambition, for all the others spring from these. Pride and arrogance make the four oldest [nuns] who are still there hateful and bitter toward each other (though otherwise they are very harmonious when it serves to the detriment of the younger [nuns]). They will not grudge anyone advantage in office, and even make an alienation from conversation and living together out of the alienation of their hearts. Yes, it has certainly been a half year that they have not come together, and spoken nothing but prickly and quarrelsome words to each other or told very annoying things about each other that are uninteresting to everyone. [They did this] even though such works themselves prove truthfully how far the desire to rule had driven the one and the other. It was not enough for them that one party made the other despised through the disclosure of their godless life in the convent, but they troubled themselves scrupulously to write letters to other convents and also to Mainz to his Electoral Grace,[3] so that he was obliged to send three [nuns] from Erfurt back to another convent that is almost one hundred miles away. Despite sending the one party away, the remaining four who are still ruling could not lay down or turn away from their pride and ambition. This is proved by the cunning invented means and slanders with which they belittle and despise those whom they presume are gaining preference over the others, making them suspect to the highest authorities and others whom they presume can do something

und verdächtig machen, darmit ja ihrer Gewaltthätigkeit und unertäglichem Hochmut nichts benommen werde.

Bey solchem Leben wollen sich die Nonnen dennoch rühmen, sie folgen im Kloster am allernähesten dem Exempel Christi. Wie fein sich aber ihr Leben mit gemeldtem Ruhme vergleiche, erscheinet weiter aus dem schändlichen Neid, den sie gegen einander haben, nicht allein bey dem Vorzuge in Aemptern, sondern in allen Sachen, und sonderlich den Natürlichen Gaben. Ist eine etwas verständiger, geschickter, in delicaten Arbeiten besser erfahren, mehr geliebet, hat bessere Freundschafft, wird ihr einiger Vorzug oder etwas besonders gegeben, es sey an Kleidung oder sonst etwas, so hat sie deßwegen fast so viel Neidhässige, als Wissenschafft darumb haben, die alle List anwenden, wie sie solche Gaben verdunckeln und fernere Recommendation und Beförderung abwenden mögen.

Daraus entspringet dann weiter das dritte so ich obgedacht, daß die jenigen, so auff solche Masse beneidet sind, auch mit unerhörten Unwarheiten verächtlich und verdächtig gemacht werden. Das Unchristlichste aber ist, daß sich etliche zusammen schlagen, und eine der anderen falsch Zeugniß gibt, diese oder jene solle solche Sachen geredet oder gethan haben, die sie wissen, daß sie ohne böse Nachrede und Straffe nicht abgehen, und also die Unschuldigen zur Züchtig- und Abstraffung bringen. Es wäre offt nicht zu verwundern, wann die auff solche Art geplagte Nonnen wegen der an ihnen verübten Unbillingkeiten für Schmertzen und Trostlosigkeit versüncken. Ich habe es erfuhren, und kan dahero desto sicherer davon schreiben und urtheilen, wie sich die armen bedrängten Seelen im Kloster-Stande befinden.

Ihrer vornehmste Obrigkeit so wol ausser als in dem Kloster, die nicht in allen nach ihrem Belieben gethan, haben sie mit übeler Nachrede nicht geschonet. Ich erwarte mit verlangen, was sie noch ferner für Gifft-Pfeile des übeln Nachredens wider mich, ihrer Gewohnheit nach, außschiessen werden: worvor Ich mich doch im wenigsten nicht fürchte, weil neben meinem guten Gewissen, noch so redliche Gemüther in und ausser dem Kloster gefunden werden, die bezeugen können, daß ich mich bey allen erlittenen Verfolgungen und Unbilligkeiten also verhalten habe, daß sie mich keines leichtsinnigen Lebens bezüchtigen können. Keine wird mich haben im Kloster hören klagen über die Strenge des Ordens, aber wol über den unmässigen Zorn, unbilliges Urtheil, unverdiente Straffe, Rasen,

about this. Nothing would stun [me] about their violence and unbelievable pride.

Through such a life the nuns still want to glorify themselves, [saying that] they follow Christ's example closest in the convent. How well their life may be compared with their supposed glory may be seen also in the shameful envy that they have for one another. Not only in preference for offices, but in all things and especially in natural gifts. If one [of them] is somewhat more intelligent, more gifted in delicate work, more experienced, more loved, has better friendships, is given a preference or something special in clothing, or something else, then she has almost as many envious haters around her as there are sciences. They apply all sorts of tricks, [telling her] how she should hide such gifts and turn away from further recommendations and promotions.

From this springs the third [thing] I have mentioned above, that those who are envied in such a way are made suspect and despised through outrageous untruths. The most unchristian, however, is that some of them smash each other to pieces, and bear false witness about the others, that this one or that one is supposed to have said or done such things. For they know, that [the others] will not leave unless there are evil slanders and punishment. Therefore they bring the innocent to correction and punishment. It is not surprising that the nuns who have been through this are engulfed in the pain and desolation caused by such unfairness. I have experienced, and therefore can certainly write about and judge, how the poor distressed souls in the clerical order find themselves.

They have not spared their distinguished authorities — both outside and inside of the convent — from this evil defamation if they didn't do all that they wanted. I long [to see] what sort of poison arrows of evil defamation they will shoot after me, as is their habit. I don't fear these in the least, because along with my good conscience, my honest soul will be found [in my actions] both inside and outside the convent. I will prove that I have behaved through all of the persecutions and unfairness, and that they can not accuse me of a frivolous life. No one has heard me complain while in the convent about the severity of the order, but certainly about the, immeasurable anger, unfair judgments, unearned punishments, the rages and furies of Dr.

und Wüthen des D. Hunolds samt den Frantzöischen Nonnen, mit
welchen sie gegen die jenige verfahren, so ihr böses Leben nicht gut
gesprochen: sonderlich die weniger als löbliche Conversation, so ein
und anderer aus den geistlichen Oberen des Klosters mit etlichen
aus den Nonnen hat, welche auch alle ihre Thun und Wercke dahin
richten, wie sie denenselben auffs beste gefallen mögen. Ein paar
Stündig ja vielmal längeres Liebes-Gespräch, dergleichen ich mit
meinen eigenen Ohren gehöret, dienet zu einer solchen Vorbereitung
zu der Meß, daß öffters die Hostien zu consecriren vergessen worden
und die verlangende ohne communion von der Kirchen weichen
müssen.

Uber solche und noch mehr dergleichen Stücke, so ich zu
Vermeydung Aergernisses mitstillschweigen übergehe, gestehe Ich
gern, habe Ich bißweilen etliche Worte, die mich darnach viel gekostet,
fahren lassen, daraus wol abzunehmen gewesen, daß ich einen solchen
Stand, darinne so ein ärgerliches Leben geführet wird, so hoch, als er
ausgegeben wird, nicht schätzen könne. Ich kan auch noch nicht
begrieffen, woher sie die Freyheit nehmen, denselben der H. Tauffe
gleich zuachten, ihn über alle andere Stände zu erheben, sich heiliger
und besser als andere Christen zu schätzen, ja für solche, welche nicht
allein für sich Vergebung der Sünden und die ewige Seligkeit durch
ihr Kloster-Leben und Menschen-Satzungen, die sie doch eben so
wenig, als das noch Nothwendigere halten, zu erlangen vermeinen,
sondern sich auch rühmen, daß sie andere ihrer Verdienste theilhafftig
machen können. Welche Opinion, solten sie auch gleich so wol leben,
als böse sie leben, dem Spruch des H. Pauli Eph. 2. v. 8 gerade zuwider
is: Aus Gnaden seyd ihr selig worden durch den Glauben, und dasselbe
nicht aus euch, GOttes Gabe ist es, nicht aus den Wercken, auf daß
sich nicht jemand rühme. Es wäre zu wünschen, daß solcher Kern-
Spruch sampt anderen etwas genauer betrachtet würde von allen den
jenigen, so ausser und in den Klöstern sich zu der Römisch-
Catholischen Kirchen bekennnen, so würden sie sich nicht so sehr
auff ihre eigene Verdienst und Wercke verlassen, mit Hindansetzung
des Verdiensts Christi unsers Heylandes, dessen man jetzo im
Pabsthum fast gäntzlich vergisset.

Gleichwie in andern Dingen von neubegierigen Gemüthern die
Neurungen geliebet werden, so geschiehet es im Pabsthum auch mit
der Religion, da sie neben dem einigen Lebens-Wege neuerlich viel
andere Nebenwege erdichten, also die Leute von dem rechten Wege

Hunolt and the French nuns, directed against those who did not speak
well of their evil life. And also about the less than praiseworthy conversations, which one or another of the spiritual directors of the convent had with some of the nuns, who adjusted all their actions so as
to please them [i.e., the spiritual directors] the best. Sometimes these
talks — which I heard with my own ears — sounded like lovers'
conversations that went on for a few hours or more. They went on
during preparations for the mass so that they [the priests] often for-
got to consecrate the host and those who wanted to take communion
had to turn away from the church.

I said a few words about such things from time to time — though
I confess I was sometimes silent in order to prevent scandal — which
cost me dearly afterwards, from which it may be concluded that I
could not value such an estate [i.e., the clerical estate], in which such
a terrible life was lived, as highly as one is supposed to. I also cannot
understand how they take the liberty to lift themselves above all other
estates, and value themselves as holier and better than other Christians, though all are equal in baptism. Yes, they hold themselves to be
[people] who can earn forgiveness of sins and eternal life not only for
themselves but also for others through their convent life and human
rules, even though they actually follow these as little as they follow
[the rules] that are more important. This idea, even if they lived it
well instead of badly, is directly opposed by the words of Saint Paul,
Ephesians 2:8: "Through grace are you saved by faith, and that not of
yourselves, but it is a gift of God, not through works, lest anyone
should boast." It is to be wished that such central words, along with
others, were regarded somewhat more closely by all of those who
confess to the Roman Catholic Church both outside and inside the
convent. Then they would not trust so much in their own works and
merit, setting aside the merit of Christ our Savior, who is now almost
completely forgotten in the papacy.

Just as in other areas where curious spirits love things that are new,
so is it now in the papacy also with religion, for alongside the one
true path, many other side paths are newly created which lead people
away from the true path and get them to place their hopes in things

abführen, und ihre Hoffnung stellen machen auff solche Dinge, die in GOttes-Wort keinen Grund haben. Und eben dieses ist die eine Ursach, die mich bewogen hat, die Evangelische Religion anzunehmen, als welche zwar vorschreibet und treibet, Christliche und schrifftmässige gute Wercke zuthun, dadurch den wahren Glauben und die Liebe gegen GOtt und den Nechsten zuerweisen, aber zu Erlangung der Seligkeit und Vergebung der Sünden die Christgläubige weiset auff daseintzige Verdienst Christi, dasselbe sich mit festem Vertrauen zuzueignen.

Die andere Motiv, so mich beweget, die Römische Kirche zuverlassen, ist, daß sie neben dem Vertrauen auff eigene Werck ihre Hoffnung und Zuversicht stellen, auff die Verdienste, Hülffe, und Vorbitte der Heiligen, denselben Kirchen auffrichten, Gelübde und solche Ehre anthun, die eigentlich und allein Gott gebühret, und damit zugleich den wahren Gottesdienst gantz vermessentlich hindansetzen. Unter hundert Kirchen im Pabstthum wird kaum eine gefunden werden die der H. Dreyfaltigkeit oder einer Person der Gottheit geweihet ist. Unter tausend Personen ist offt nicht eine die ihre Zuflucht, in was Nöten und Anliegen es auch seyn möchte, nehmen zu Christo dem einigen Nothhelffer und Mittler zwichen GOtt und den Menschen, sondern alle wenden sich von ihm zu gewissen Heiligen, von denen hoffen und erwarten sie Hülffe, schreiben auch die empfangene Hülffe denselben Heiligen, oder doch deren Vorbitte zu, die sie darum angeruffen. Wie fein reymet sich solches abermal mit der Schrifft darinnen Gott Ps. 50. v. 15. befiehlet Ruff mich an in der Noth, so wil ich doch erretten, so solt du mich preisen, und 1. Tim. 2. v. 5. Glich wie nur ein Gott, also auch nur ein Mittler zwischen Gott und den Menschen ist, nemlich der Mensch Christus Jesus, der sich selbst für uns gegeben hat. Worbey mir dann gleichfals wolgefället, daß in der Evangelischen Religion gelehret wird, man solle der Heiligen so wol zur Nachfolge ihres Glaubens als Gottseligen Lebens Ehrerbietig gedencken, daß also diese alleinseligmachende Religion fälschlich bezüchiget wird, als lehre sie, die Mutter Gottes und Heiligen schenden und unehren.

Die dritte Ursach meiner Religions Aenderung rühret her von der Verwirrung der Papistische Lehre in den Glaubens Artikulen, vom Ablaß, Beicht, und Fegfeuer, welche mir von langer Zeit her viel Nachdenckens verursachet hat, weil das eine klar wieder das andere lauffet. Eines theils lehret man im Pabsthum, der Ablaß nehme alle

for which there is no justification in God's Word. This is the reason I have decided to join the evangelical religion, which prescribes and orders us to do Christian good works in accordance with the commandments, through which we show true faith and love toward God and our neighbor. But we Christians point to the sole merit of Christ for the achievement of holiness and the forgiveness of sins, and accept this in firm trust.

The other motive that moved me to leave the Roman Church is that along with trust in their own works, they place hope and confidence in the merits, help, and supplications of the saints of their church, make vows and give similar honors to them that belong only to God, and at the same time completely presumptuously set aside the true worship service. Out of a hundred churches in Catholicism will scarcely one be found that is dedicated to the Holy Trinity or one of the persons of the Godhead. Out of a thousand people there is often not one who takes his refuge — whatever their needs or desires are — in Christ who is the only aid and intercessor between God and humans. They all turn from him to certain saints, hoping and waiting for help. They also write that they have received help from the saints they have called upon, or through their intercession. How does this fit with Scripture, where God commands in Psalm 50:15: "Call on me in your need; I will deliver you, and you shall glorify me." And in 1 Timothy 2:5: "Just as there is only one God, there is only one intercessor between God and humans, that is, the man Jesus Christ, who gave himself for us." It also then similarly pleases me, that it is taught in the evangelical religion, that one should regard the saints as honorable and imitate their faith and blessed lives. This religion, which alone makes one sanctified, is falsely accused of teaching that one should dishonor and defame the mother of God and the saints.

The third reason that I changed my religion is the confusion of papist teachings in the articles of faith about indulgences, penance, and purgatory, which have caused me to think about these for a long time, because one [teaching] clearly contradicts the other. On one hand, it is taught in the papacy that indulgences take away all tempo-

zeitliche Straffen, so wegen der Sünden auszustehen, hinweg. Nun kan man desselben unbeschreiblich viel erlangen. Für kleine Gebete, und etliche Ave Maria sind viel tausend Jahr Ablaß ertheilet. Wolte nun jemand sorgfältig seyn, viel Ablaß zu erlangen, so könte er in einer geringen Zeit desselben auff eine solche Anzahl Jahre bekommen, welche weiter hinauß reichen werden, als etwan diese Zeitlichkeit wehren wird. Soll nun, wie sie vorgeben, das Fegfeuer länger nicht als biß an den Jüngsten Tag wehren, worzu dienet dann der auff so viel tausend Jahre drüber erlagte Ablaß? Weiter kan eine solche Summa Ablaß zusammen gebracht erden, die die Straffe nach ihre Lehre weit übertrifft. Wann nun der Ablaß solche wegnimmet, was ist dann nöthig, daß sie lehren, man müste durch Fasten und andere eusserliche Bußwercke für die Sünde gnug thun, und wann solches hier nicht geschehe, würde das übrige im Fegfeuer abzubüssen verbleiben? Allen, die in ihren letzen Zügen den Heiligen Namen Jesus und Maria außsprechen, ist vollkommener Ablaß verliehen, welcher alle übrige Straffe auffheben sol. Ist nun dem also, was beten sie dann weiter nach dem Tode für solche Seelen? Denn so der Anlaß alle Straffe hinweg genommen, worvor solten sie dann weiter im Fegfeuer auffgehalten werden? Zum wenigsten ist nicht nothwendig, daß so viel Geld für Seel-Messen ausgegeben wird, wann man durch wenige Gebete auff so viel tausend Jahr Ablaß erlangen kan. Weiter, wann der Ablaß und Beicht, nach der Lehre im Pabstum, die Würckung hat, das jener alle zeitliche Straffe, diese aber die Schuld hinnimmet, so kan man sich ja seiner Seligkeit unzweyfelich versichern? Und solches wollen sie doch nicht zulassen. Ob nun dieses nicht ein wahrer Irrgarten der Gewissen sey, lasse ich einen jeden urtheilen. Welches aber kein Wunder. Dann wo man einmal von dem geoffenbarten, klaren und reinen Worte Gottes abweichet, so kan man nichtanders als in Finsterniß wandeln.

Unter andern ist merckwürdig, da sie ohne allen Grund der H. Canonischen Schrifft ein Fegfeuer erdichten, und solches anders nicht als mit Fabeln und Teuffels-Verblendungen bestätigen, daß dergleichen auch vor nunmehr ohngefehr zweyen Jahren sich in dem Kloster, darinne ich mich auffgehalten, begeben. Da war zu hören grosses Getümmel und Poltern an unterschiedlichen Orten, es wurden einer Magd durch Geister besondere Sachen eröffnet, die sie den Nonnen sagen liessen. An mir hatte den Teufelischen Geistern mißfallen, daß ich öffters in unserm Kloster-Garten den Lutherischen Gesängen in

ral punishments that arise out of sin. One can accomplish unbeliev-ably much through these. For little prayers and a few Ave Marias, many thousand years of indulgences are handed out. If one is careful and receives many indulgences, so can one in a short time receive such a large number of years, that these would reach further than all time. If, as they say, purgatory will not last any longer than Judgment Day, what use is it to receive indulgences that are so many thousand years longer? Further, such an amount of indulgences can be brought together that far exceeds the punishment set by their teachings. If indulgences take this [the need for punishment] away, why is it then necessary, as they teach, that one must do more to take away one's sins through fasting and other acts of penance, and if one doesn't do this here [on earth] the rest will remain to be atoned for in purgatory? Everyone that utters the holy names Jesus and Mary in their last breath is promised complete indulgence which lifts all other punishments. If this is true, why do they continue to pray for such souls after they have died? If indulgences have taken away all punishments, why are they then stopped in purgatory? At the least it is not necessary to give so much money for masses for the dead, if one can receive so many thousand years of indulgences for a few prayers. And further, if indul-gences and penance, according to the teaching in the papacy, have the result that for these all temporal punishments are lifted and for those the guilt is lifted, shouldn't one be able to secure one's salvation without a doubt? This [teaching] they still won't accept. If this isn't a true garden of error for the conscience, I'll let everyone judge for themselves. No wonder. For once one turns away from the revealed, clear, and true Word of God, one can walk in nothing but darkness.

Among other things, it is remarkable that they invent purgatory, without any basis for this in holy canonical Scripture, and defend this with nothing other than stories and the devil's delusions. Things like this [happened] about two years ago in the convent where I had gone to stay: There was a loud turmoil and rumbling in different places, and a maid told the nuns that certain things had been revealed to her through spirits. The devil's spirits were displeased with me, because I often listened to Lutheran hymns from the church when I was in the convent garden.[4] They gave as a sign a hand that had been burned on

der Regular-Kirchen zugehöret. Sie gaben zum Zeichen eine in Papier gebrante Hand, und dergleichen mehr, darmit sie glaubend machten, es wären Seelen, so wegen verblibener Straffe nun, wie sie sageten, über 40. Jahr in der andern Welt auffgehalten worden. Es wurden deßwegen viel Messen gelesen, Fasten, und viel andere Buß-wercke geschahen zu ihrer Erlösung. Was aber dieses für Lügen-Geister gewest sind, hat der Außgang gewiesen. Als die Nonnen nach lang gehabter Hoffnung den von den Geisteren versprochenen Schatz im Garten zu überkommen vermeynten, gieng der Magd, welcher sich die Geister allezeit offenbahreten, auß dem Kloster weg, und begab sich an einen Evangelischen Ort, allda sie wider die allein seligmachende Religion annahm, von welcher sie zuvor durch der Jesuiten Geschenke zum Pabsthum war verführet worden, da hat sie bekennet, daß der leidige Satan durch solche Verblendung sie von ihrem Vorsatz, den sie gehabt, nach Antrieb ihres Gewisses sich wider zu der Evangelischen Religion zubegeben, abwenden wollen. Anfangs hätte sie sich zwar lassen bethören, die Lehre des Fegfeuers zu glauben, aber bald hernach hätte sie gnugsamerkennet, daß es eine lautere List und Betrug des Teuffels sey, daher sie dann darauff ihr Vorhaben wegen wider Annehmung der vorher verlassen, sondern mich auch zur Beständigkeit in derselben ermahnen. Solte Sie aber noch gleichwol über verhoffen einig Mißfallen daran tragen, daß ich solches ohne ihren vorbewust und Einwilligung vorgenommen, so wolle Sie bedencken, was mehrbesagter mein Beichtvater Herr P. Marcus Schönemann in seinem Catholischen Zeughause p. 236 beweglich an-und mit Zeugnisse H. Schrifft stattlich ausführet, daß man sich durch die difficultäten, die von Eltern, Brüdern, Schwestern, oder anderen Angehörigen gemachet werden, nicht solle abhalten lassen, zu der fürwahr und seligmachend erkanten Religion zu wenden, und daß Gott dem Herrn zum höchsten mißfalle die Forchtsam: und Kleinmütigkeit in Sachen die unsere Seligkeit angehen.

Hoffe also und bitte Kindlich, die Frau Mutter beliebe mich deßwegen zu excusiren, und mir noch ferner mit dero Mütterlichen Hulde zugethan zu verbleiben, welche ich hiermit in Gottes gnädige Schutz befehle und biß ins Grad verbleibe.

Meiner Hochgeehrten Frau Mutter Gotha 21. Jan. A. 1678
demüthigst und gehorsamste Tochter Martha Elisabeth Zitterinn.

a piece of paper and more things like that through which they wanted to make [people] believe that these were souls which had been stopped in the other world for over forty years because of their remaining punishments. For this reason many masses were read and fasts and other acts of penance performed for their salvation. The results of this pointed out what sort of lying spirits these were. As the nuns were supposed to receive the treasure in the garden which had been long promised them by the spirits, the maid who had received the revelations from the spirits went away out of the convent, and went to an evangelical place. She accepted the only religion which saves one [i.e., Protestantism] again, from which she had been led astray by the Jesuits, the gift to the papacy. She admitted that the disagreeable Satan wanted to turn her away with such delusions from her intention — caused by the force of her conscience — of returning to the evangelical religion. At the beginning she had let herself begin to believe the teachings about purgatory, but shortly after that she understood well enough that it was only lies and a deceit of the devil. After that she [returned to] her intention of taking up again that which she had left, and also admonished me to constancy in this. In case she bears [ill-feelings] because of the possible displeasure which might result because I have presented this without her agreement or foreknowledge, she should think about what my former confessor, Herr Pastor Marcus Schönemann, in his *Catholischen Zeughaus*, p. 236, sets out with feeling and with many examples from Holy Scripture: That one should not let oneself be held back from turning to the true, salvation-bringing religion by the difficulties that can be presented by parents, brothers, sisters or other relatives. God the Lord is greatly displeased by timidity and despondency in things that pertain to our salvation.

I therefore hope and request in a childlike manner, that you, my mother, will choose to excuse me for these reasons, and that your motherly favors will remain attached to me. I recommend you to God's gracious protection and remain until I am in my grave, your humble and obedient daughter, Martha Elisabeth Zitter.

To my highly honored mother,
Gotha, January 21, 1678

Dem geneigtem Leser wird hiemit vermeldet, daß hinter dem
fälschlich also titulirten Unüberwindtlichem Catholischen Zeughause,
so zu Erffurt bey Johann Bernhard Michaeln neulichst gedrucket,
und heute allhie zum Vorschein kommen, ein Posscriptum (soll
Postscriptum heissen) eines Sendschreibens Herrn Andreæ
Wunderlichs, Bürgern zu Würtzburg, an Herrn Petrum Wahrenfels,
Bürgern zu Erffurt, und dessen Beantwortung zu finden. Diese
Beantwortung betrifft die Jungfer Zitterinn, eine Urheberin dieses
an ihre Frau Mutter abgelassenen und nachdem es zu Gotha bey Hn.
Christoph Reihern in kurtzer Frist dreymahl gedrucket allhie bey Hn.
Johann Gollnern zum vierdtenmahl auffgelegten Schriebens. Der
unter Petri Wahrenfels Nahmen liegende Meister verdienet solche
Benahmungen mit nichten, und könte derselbe mit gutem Fug
Bencotsba, Filius Mendacii, Lügenkind oder auch Lügenfels genennet
werden, weil seine Schrifft mit so vielen Handgreifflichen Unwarheiten
angefüllet, daß man wol mit H.P. Marco Schönemann pag. 61 dieses
Unüberwindlichen Catholischen Zeughauses sagen möchte: Ich wil
versichern, wenn ein dieser Sachen kündiger Leser nicht das
Balsambüchslein wird gebrauchen, so wirds ihm übel gehen; in dem
ein so sehr garstiger Gestanck, und nicht weniger als in dem von P.
Schönemann angezogenem Evangelischen Wetterhahn, aus demselben
herauß hauchet. Gedulde dich aber nur ein weniges, geliebter Leser,
und glaube festiglich, daß weil die Ursuliner Nonnen und ihre
Helffers-Helffer wider die Gott und Ehrliebende Junger Zitterin zu
toben nicht aufhören wollen, ihnen auch durch rechtschaffene und
auf der unfehlbaren Warheit gegründete Schriften derogestalt soll
begegnet werden, daß sie wünschen möchten, dergleichen Spiel
nimmer angefangen zu haben. Der grosse Gott wird gewiß und
warhafftig den Satan unter seine Füsse treten, und ferner zu Spott
und Schanden machen, die seine heilige Ehre verkleinern, die
Evangelische Warheit verlästern, und die Lutherische Gemeine in
Erffurt ohne eintzige Ursach drücken und ängsten wollen. Geschrieben
Jena den II. Martii 1678.

[Postscript]
It is reported to the well-disposed reader, that at the end of the falsely titled *Unüberwindtlichem Catholischen Zeughause,* that has recently been printed by Johann Bernhard Michael at Erfurt, and has appeared here today, is a "posscript" (which should have been titled "postscript"), a letter from Herr Andrew Wunderlich, a citizen of Würzburg, to Herr Peter Wahrenfels, a citizen of Erfurt, and the latter's answer. This answer concerns the writings of Miss Zitter to her mother, which have been printed recently three times by Herr Christopher Reiher at Gotha and for a fourth time here by Herr Johann Gollner. The example which is [printed] under Herr Peter Wahrenfels' name does nothing to earn such a title [i.e., as an edition] and can certainly with good cause be called a little liar, a lying stone. His writings are filled with so many tangible untruths that one can say along with Herr Pastor Marcus Schönemann on page 61 of *Unüberwindtlichem Catholischen Zeughause*: "I will insure that when a reader who is knowledgable about these things does not want to use a balsam-pillow [as a pomodor] it will go badly for him." There will be such a nasty stink, not less than that which breathed out of the *Evangelischen Wetterhahn* to which Pastor Schönemann was referring. Have patience a little while, dear reader, and firmly believe, that because the Ursuline nuns and their helpers' helpers will not stop raving against the God- and honor-loving Miss Zitter, they shall be met to such a degree by righteous writings which are grounded in the unmistakable truth that they will wish that they had never started with this game. The great God will certainly and truly tread Satan under his feet and bring into shame and mockery those who diminish his holy honor, slander the evangelical truth, and seek to oppress and alarm the Lutheran congregation in Erfurt without any cause. Written in Jena, March 2, 1678.[5]

Notes

1. In early modern German, an "-in" ending was often added to a woman's family name in order to indicate that the individual was female. This is no longer the practice for proper names in modern German, though it remains the practice for most occupational titles, such as student (*der Student, die Studentin*) or teacher (*der Lehrer, die Lehrerin*). Because the -in ending is no longer used in modern German, Zitter's name is given without it in the English translation.

2. The word "Corban" appears in both the German and English Bibles and means "given to God" or "an offering." In the Gospel of Mark (7:11-12) Jesus quotes the Pharisees, saying: "but you say, 'If a man tell his father or his mother, What you would have gained from me is Corban' (that is, given to God) — and then you no longer permit him to do anything for his father and mother." Zitter is here implying that the nuns are acting like Pharisees in urging girls to offer themselves to God in opposition to their parents' wishes.

3. The Bishop of Mainz, who had charge over Catholic convents in this area, was one of the electors in the Holy Roman Empire, and so is here referred to by that title.

4. The convent was located in an area of Germany that was officially Lutheran at that time, so services outside of the convent, including those in the church near the convent walls, were Lutheran, not Catholic.

5. This postscript is unsigned, and appears to have been added by Zitter's printer explaining why he was now coming out with a fourth edition of her pamphlet. (He also refers to this on the title-page, noting that this was printed "for the fourth time to avert much scandal.") Zitter herself may have also had a hand in this, however, for, just as in the body of the text, the words of her Catholic former confessor, Pastor Schönemann, are tipped on their head and used to argue for a Protestant position.